crockpot™

Slow Cooker

RECIPES

Publications International, Ltd.

Pictured on the front cover: Black Bean, Zucchini and Corn Enchiladas *(page 124)*

Pictured on the back cover *(clockwise from top left):* Miso-Poached Salmon *(page 88),* Boneless Pork Roast with Garlic *(page 64),* Hot Beef Sandwiches au Jus *(page 142),* Bolognese over Rigatoni *(page 103)* and Matzo Ball Soup *(page 25).*

ISBN: 978-1-63938-388-7

Manufactured in China.

8 7 6 5 4 3 2 1

Microwave Cooking: Microwave ovens vary in wattage. Use the cooking times as guidelines and check for doneness before adding more time.

Contents

Slow Cooking 101

Slow Cooker Sizes

Smaller **Crockpot**™ slow cookers—such as 1- to 3½-quart models—are the perfect size for cooking for singles, a couple or empty-nesters (and also for serving dips).

While medium-size **Crockpot**™ slow cookers (those holding somewhere between 3 quarts and 5 quarts) will easily cook enough food at a time to feed a small family, they're also convenient for holiday side dishes or appetizers.

Large **Crockpot**™ slow cookers are great for large family dinners, holiday entertaining and potluck suppers. A 6- to 7-quart model is ideal if you like to make meals in advance, or have dinner tonight and store leftovers for another day.

Types of Slow Cookers

Current **Crockpot**™ slow cookers come equipped with many different features and benefits, from auto cook programs to stovetop-safe stoneware to timed programming. Visit **www.crock-pot.com** to find the **Crockpot**™ slow cooker that best suits your needs.

How you plan to use a **Crockpot**™ slow cooker may affect the model you choose to purchase. For everyday cooking, choose a size large enough to serve your family. If you plan to use the **Crockpot**™ slow cooker primarily for entertaining, choose one of the larger sizes. Basic **Crockpot**™ slow cookers can hold as little as 16 ounces or as much as 7 quarts. The smallest sizes are great for keeping dips warm on a buffet, while the larger sizes can more readily fit large quantities of food and larger roasts.

Cooking, Stirring and Food Safety

Crockpot™ slow cookers are safe to leave unattended. The outer heating base may get hot as it cooks, but it should not pose a fire hazard. The heating element in the heating base functions at a low wattage and is safe for your countertops.

Your **Crockpot**™ slow cooker should be filled about one-half to three-fourths full for most recipes unless otherwise instructed. Lean meats such as chicken or pork tenderloin will cook faster than meats with more connective tissue and fat such as beef chuck or pork shoulder. Bone-in meats will take longer than boneless cuts. Typical **Crockpot**™ slow cooker dishes take approximately 7 to 8 hours to reach the simmer point on LOW and about 3 to 4 hours on HIGH. Once the vegetables and meat start to simmer and braise, their flavors will fully blend and meat will become fall-off-the-bone tender.

According to the USDA, all bacteria are killed at a temperature of 165°F. It's important to follow the recommended cooking times and not to open the lid often, especially early in the cooking process when heat is building up inside the unit. If you need to open the lid to check on your food or are adding additional ingredients, remember to allow additional cooking time if necessary to ensure food is cooked through and tender.

Large **Crockpot**™ slow cookers, the 6- to 7-quart sizes, may benefit with a quick stir halfway through cook time to help distribute heat and promote even cooking. It's usually unnecessary to stir at all, as even ½ cup liquid will help to distribute heat, and the stoneware is the perfect medium for holding food at an even temperature throughout the cooking process.

Oven-Safe

All **Crockpot**™ slow cooker removable stoneware inserts may (without their lids) be used safely in ovens at up to 400°F. Also, all **Crockpot**™ slow cookers are microwavable without their lids. If you own another brand of slow cooker, please refer to your owner's manual for specific stoneware cooking medium tolerances.

Frozen Food

Frozen food or partially frozen food can be successfully cooked in a **Crockpot**™ slow cooker; however, it will require longer cooking time than the same recipe made with fresh food. It's almost always preferable to thaw frozen food prior to placing it in the **Crockpot**™ slow cooker. Using an instant-read thermometer is recommended to ensure meat is fully cooked through.

Pasta and Rice

If you're converting a recipe that calls for uncooked pasta, cook the pasta on the stovetop just until slightly tender before adding to the **Crockpot**™ slow cooker. If you are converting a recipe that calls for cooked rice, stir in raw rice with other ingredients; add ¼ cup extra liquid per ¼ cup of raw rice.

Beans

Beans must be softened completely before combining with sugar and/or acidic foods. Sugar and acid have a hardening effect on beans and will prevent softening. Fully cooked canned beans may be used as a substitute for dried beans.

Vegetables

Root vegetables often cook more slowly than meat. Cut vegetables accordingly to cook at the same rate as meat—large versus small, or lean versus marbled—and place near the sides or bottom of the stoneware to facilitate cooking.

Herbs

Fresh herbs add flavor and color when added at the end of the cooking cycle; if added at the beginning, many fresh herbs' flavor will dissipate over long cook times. Ground and/or dried herbs and spices work well in slow cooking and may be added at the beginning, and for dishes with shorter cook times, hearty fresh herbs such as rosemary and thyme hold up well. The flavor power of all herbs and spices can vary greatly depending on their particular strength and shelf life. Use chili powders and garlic powder sparingly, as these can sometimes intensify over the long cook times. Always taste the finished dish and correct seasonings including salt and pepper.

Liquids

It is not necessary to use more than ½ to 1 cup liquid in most instances since juices in meats and vegetables are retained more in slow cooking than in conventional cooking. Excess liquid can be cooked down and concentrated after slow cooking on the stovetop or by removing meat and vegetables from the stoneware, stirring in one of the following thickeners, and setting the slow cooker to HIGH. Cook on HIGH for approximately 15 minutes or until juices are thickened.

Flour: All-purpose flour is often used to thicken soups or stews. Stir cold water into the flour in a small bowl until smooth. With the **Crockpot**™ slow cooker on HIGH, whisk the flour mixture into the liquid in the **Crockpot**™ slow cooker. Cover; cook on HIGH 15 minutes or until the mixture is thickened.

Cornstarch: Cornstarch gives sauces a clear, shiny appearance; it's used most often for sweet dessert sauces and stir-fry sauces. Stir cold water into the cornstarch in a small bowl until the cornstarch dissolves. Quickly stir this mixture into the liquid in the **Crockpot**™ slow cooker; the sauce will thicken as soon as the liquid boils. Cornstarch breaks down with too much heat, so never add it at the beginning of the slow cooking process, and turn off the heat as soon as the sauce thickens.

Arrowroot: Arrowroot (or arrowroot flour) comes from the root of a tropical plant that is dried and ground to a powder; it produces a thick, clear sauce. Those who are allergic to wheat often use it in place of flour. Place arrowroot in a small bowl or cup and stir in cold water until the mixture is smooth. Quickly stir this mixture into the liquid in the **Crockpot**™ slow cooker. Arrowroot thickens below the boiling point, so it even works well in a **Crockpot**™ slow cooker on LOW. Too much stirring can break down an arrowroot mixture.

Tapioca: Tapioca is a starchy substance extracted from the root of the cassava plant. Its greatest advantage is that it withstands long cooking, making it an ideal choice for slow cooking. Add it at the beginning of cooking and you'll get a clear, thickened sauce in the finished dish. Dishes using tapioca as a thickener are best cooked on the LOW setting; tapioca may become stringy when boiled for a long time.

Milk

Milk, cream and sour cream break down during extended cooking. When possible, add them during the last 15 to 30 minutes of cooking, until just heated through. Condensed soups may be substituted for milk and can cook for extended times.

Fish

Fish is delicate and should be stirred in gently during the last 15 to 30 minutes of cooking time. Cover and cook just until cooked through and serve immediately.

Baked Goods

If you wish to prepare bread, cakes or pudding cakes in a **Crockpot**™ slow cooker, you may want to purchase a covered, vented metal cake pan accessory for your **Crockpot**™ slow cooker. You can also use any straight-sided soufflé dish or deep cake pan that will fit into the stoneware of your unit. Baked goods can be prepared directly in the stoneware; however, they can be a little difficult to remove from the insert, so follow the recipe directions carefully.

Breakfast & Brunch

Apple-Almond Oatmeal

makes 6 servings

3 cups water

2 cups chopped peeled apples

1½ cups steel-cut or old-fashioned oats

¼ cup sliced almonds

½ teaspoon ground cinnamon, plus additional for garnish

¼ teaspoon salt

Brown sugar

Sliced apples (optional)

1. Combine water, chopped apples, oats, almonds, ½ teaspoon cinnamon and salt in **Crockpot**™ slow cooker. Cover; cook on LOW 8 hours.

2. Serve with brown sugar, additional cinnamon and sliced apples, if desired.

9

French Toast Bread Pudding

makes 6 to 8 servings

2 tablespoons packed dark
   brown sugar

2½ teaspoons ground cinnamon

1 loaf (24 ounces) Texas toast-
   style bread*

2 cups whipping cream

2 cups half-and-half

1¼ cups granulated sugar

4 egg yolks

2 teaspoons vanilla

¼ teaspoon salt

¼ teaspoon ground nutmeg
   Whipped cream (optional)

*If unavailable, cut day-old 24-ounce
loaf of white sandwich bread into
1-inch-thick slices.*

1. Coat inside of **Crockpot**™ slow cooker with nonstick cooking spray. Combine brown sugar and cinnamon in small bowl. Reserve 1 tablespoon; set aside.

2. Cut bread slices in half diagonally. Arrange bread slices in single layer in bottom of **Crockpot**™ slow cooker. Sprinkle rounded tablespoon of cinnamon-sugar over bread. Repeat layering with remaining bread and cinnamon-sugar.

3. Whisk cream, half-and-half, granulated sugar, egg yolks, vanilla and salt in large bowl.

4. Pour cream mixture over bread; press bread down lightly. Sprinkle reserved cinnamon-sugar over top. Cover; cook on LOW 3 to 4 hours or on HIGH 1½ to 2 hours or until toothpick inserted into center comes out clean.

5. Turn off heat. Uncover and let pudding stand 10 minutes. Serve with whipped cream, if desired.

Hash Brown and Spinach Breakfast Casserole

makes 6 to 8 servings

- **4 cups frozen southern-style diced hash browns**
- **3 tablespoons butter**
- **1 large onion, chopped**
- **2 cups (8 ounces) sliced mushrooms**
- **3 cloves garlic, minced**
- **1 package (10 ounces) frozen chopped spinach, thawed and squeezed dry**
- **8 eggs**
- **1 cup milk**
- **1 teaspoon salt**
- **¼ teaspoon black pepper**
- **1½ cups (6 ounces) shredded sharp Cheddar cheese, divided**

1. Coat inside of **Crockpot**™ slow cooker with nonstick cooking spray. Place hash browns in **Crockpot**™ slow cooker.

2. Melt butter in large skillet over medium-high heat. Add onion, mushrooms and garlic; cook 4 to 5 minutes or until onion is just starting to brown, stirring occasionally. Add spinach; cook and stir 2 minutes or until mushrooms are tender. Stir spinach mixture into hash browns in **Crockpot**™ slow cooker until combined.

3. Whisk eggs, milk, salt and pepper in large bowl until well blended. Pour over hash brown mixture in **Crockpot**™ slow cooker. Top with 1 cup cheese. Cover; cook on LOW 4 to 4½ hours or on HIGH 1½ to 2 hours or until eggs are set. Top with remaining ½ cup cheese. Cut into wedges to serve.

Overnight Breakfast Porridge

makes 4 servings

¾ **cup steel-cut oats**

¼ **cup uncooked quinoa, rinsed and drained**

¼ **cup dried cranberries, plus additional for serving**

¼ **cup raisins**

3 **tablespoons ground flax seeds**

2 **tablespoons chia seeds**

¼ **teaspoon ground cinnamon**

2½ **cups almond milk, plus additional for serving**

Maple syrup

¼ **cup sliced almonds, toasted***

*To toast almonds, spread in single layer in heavy skillet. Cook and stir over medium heat 1 to 2 minutes or until nuts are lightly browned.

1. Combine oats, quinoa, ¼ cup cranberries, raisins, flax seeds, chia seeds and cinnamon in heat-safe bowl that fits inside of 5- or 6-quart **Crockpot**™ slow cooker. Stir in 2½ cups almond milk.

2. Place bowl in **Crockpot**™ slow cooker; pour in enough water to come halfway up side of bowl.

3. Cover; cook on LOW 8 hours. Carefully remove bowl from **Crockpot**™ slow cooker. Stir in additional almond milk, if desired. Top each serving with maple syrup, almonds and additional cranberries.

Cranberry Orange Scones

makes 6 servings

¼ cup (½ stick) cold butter
1 cup plus 2 tablespoons
　 self-rising flour, divided
¾ cup buttermilk
2 teaspoons granulated sugar
¼ cup dried cranberries
1½ teaspoons orange peel, divided
½ teaspoon ground cinnamon
¼ cup powdered sugar
1½ teaspoons orange juice
⅛ teaspoon salt

1. Cut one 16-inch piece of parchment paper; fold in half crosswise. Fit parchment paper into bottom and partly up sides of 1½-quart **Crockpot™** slow cooker. Coat parchment paper with nonstick cooking spray.

2. Grate cold butter on large holes of box grater into medium bowl. Add 1 cup flour, buttermilk and granulated sugar; stir just until dry ingredients are moistened. *Do not overmix.* Combine cranberries, 1 teaspoon orange peel and cinnamon in small bowl; toss to coat. Fold cranberry mixture into dough.

3. Sprinkle work surface with remaining 2 tablespoons flour. Place dough on work surface; knead a few times until dough forms a ball. Press into 6-inch disc; score into six wedges. Place disc into **Crockpot™** slow cooker on top of parchment paper.

4. Lay a clean kitchen towel across top of **Crockpot™** slow cooker; cover with lid. Cover; cook on HIGH 1½ hours. Remove scones with parchment paper to wire rack.

5. Combine powdered sugar, orange juice, remaining ½ teaspoon orange peel and salt in small bowl; whisk until blended. Drizzle over scones. Cut along score lines into wedges; serve warm or at room temperature.

Cheese Grits with Chiles and Bacon

makes 4 servings

6 slices bacon

1 jalapeño or serrano pepper, seeded and minced*

1 large shallot or small onion, finely chopped

4 cups chicken broth

1 cup grits**

Salt and black pepper

1 cup (4 ounces) shredded Cheddar cheese

½ cup half-and-half

2 tablespoons finely chopped green onion

*Jalapeño peppers can sting and irritate the skin, so wear rubber gloves when handling peppers and do not touch your eyes.

**Use coarse, instant, yellow or stone-ground grits.

1. Heat medium skillet over medium heat. Add bacon; cook and stir until crisp. Remove to paper towel-lined plate using tongs. Chop two slices of bacon; place in **Crockpot**™ slow cooker. Chop remaining bacon; refrigerate until ready to serve.

2. Drain all but 1 tablespoon bacon drippings from skillet. Heat skillet over medium-high heat. Add jalapeño pepper and shallot; cook and stir 3 minutes or until shallot is lightly browned. Remove to **Crockpot**™ slow cooker. Stir broth, grits, salt and black pepper into **Crockpot**™ slow cooker. Cover; cook on LOW 4 hours.

3. Stir in cheese and half-and-half. Scoop into bowls; top each serving with reserved bacon and green onion. Serve immediately.

Overnight Bacon, Sourdough, Egg and Cheese Casserole

makes 6 servings

1 loaf (about 12 ounces) sourdough bread, cut into ¾-inch cubes

8 slices thick-cut bacon, chopped

1 large onion, chopped

1 medium red bell pepper, chopped

1 medium green bell pepper, chopped

2 teaspoons dried oregano

¼ cup sun-dried tomatoes packed in oil, drained and chopped

1½ cups (6 ounces) shredded sharp Cheddar cheese, divided

10 eggs

1 cup milk

1 teaspoon salt

¾ teaspoon black pepper

1. Coat inside of **Crockpot**™ slow cooker with nonstick cooking spray. Add bread.

2. Heat large skillet over medium heat. Add bacon; cook and stir until crisp. Remove bacon to paper towel-lined plate using slotted spoon.

3. Pour off all but 1 tablespoon of drippings from skillet. Heat skillet over medium heat. Add onion, bell peppers and oregano; cook 5 to 7 minutes or until onion is softened, stirring occasionally. Stir in sun-dried tomatoes; cook 1 minute. Pour over bread in **Crockpot**™ slow cooker. Stir in bacon and 1 cup cheese.

4. Whisk eggs, milk, salt and black pepper in large bowl until well blended; pour over bread mixture in **Crockpot**™ slow cooker. Press down on bread to allow bread mixture to absorb egg mixture. Sprinkle remaining ½ cup cheese over top. Cover; cook on LOW 6 to 8 hours or on HIGH 3 to 4 hours. Cut into squares to serve.

Savory Sausage Bread Pudding

makes 4 to 6 servings

4 eggs

2 cups milk

½ teaspoon salt

¼ teaspoon black pepper

¼ teaspoon dried thyme

⅛ teaspoon red pepper flakes

1 package (12 ounces) smoked breakfast sausage links, cut into ½-inch pieces

¾ cup (3 ounces) shredded Cheddar cheese

2 cups cubed day-old bread (½-inch cubes)

1 tablespoon butter, softened

1. Prepare foil handles.* Whisk eggs in large bowl until well blended. Stir in milk, salt, black pepper, thyme and red pepper flakes. Add sausage, cheese and bread; press bread into egg mixture. Let stand 10 minutes or until liquid is absorbed.

2. Butter 2-quart baking dish that fits inside of **Crockpot**™ slow cooker. Pour sausage mixture into baking dish. Cover dish with buttered foil, butter side down.

3. Pour 1 inch of hot water into **Crockpot**™ slow cooker. Add baking dish. Cover; cook on LOW 4 to 5 hours or until toothpick inserted into center comes out clean. Remove dish using foil handles. Let stand 10 minutes before serving.

*Prepare foil handles by tearing off one 18-inch long piece of foil; fold in half lengthwise. Fold in half lengthwise again to create 18×3-inch strip. Repeat two times. Crisscross foil strips in spoke design; place in **Crockpot**™ slow cooker. Leave strips in during cooking so you can easily lift the cooked item out again when cooking is complete.

Soups & Stews

Matzo Ball Soup
makes 4 to 6 servings

Soup

- **12 cups chicken broth**
- **4 parsnips, sliced into ½-inch rounds**
- **2 carrots, sliced into ½-inch rounds**
- **3 leeks, sliced**
- **1 large onion, sliced**
- **1 small rotisserie chicken (optional)**
- **1 tablespoon fresh dill**
- **Salt and black pepper**

Matzo Balls

- **4 eggs**
- **1¼ cups matzo meal**
- **½ cup water**
- **5 tablespoons butter, melted**
- **1 small bunch fresh Italian parsley, minced**
- **1 tablespoon minced fresh sage**
- **Salt and black pepper**

1. Combine broth, parsnips, carrots, leeks and onion in **Crockpot**™ slow cooker. Cover; cook on LOW 8 to 10 hours or on HIGH 4 to 5 hours.

2. For matzo balls, whisk eggs in large bowl until blended. Stir in matzo meal, water, butter, parsley, sage, salt and pepper. Roll into 1½-inch balls or smaller; place on baking sheet. Cover and refrigerate 30 minutes to 1 hour.

3. Bring large saucepan of salted water to a boil. Add matzo balls. Reduce heat; simmer 20 minutes. Remove with slotted spoon and reserve until needed.

4. If desired, remove skin and bones from chicken; cut into bite-sized pieces. Add chicken, dill and matzo balls to soup. Cover; cook on HIGH 15 minutes or until heated through. Season with salt and pepper.

Roasted Tomato-Basil Soup

makes 6 servings

2 cans (28 ounces *each*) whole tomatoes, drained, 3 cups liquid reserved

2½ tablespoons packed dark brown sugar

1 medium onion, finely chopped

3 cups vegetable broth

3 tablespoons tomato paste

¼ teaspoon ground allspice

1 can (5 ounces) evaporated milk

¼ cup shredded fresh basil (about 10 large leaves), plus additional for garnish

Salt and black pepper

1. Preheat oven to 450°F. Line baking sheet with foil; spray with nonstick cooking spray. Arrange tomatoes on foil in single layer. Sprinkle with brown sugar; top with onion. Bake 25 minutes or until tomatoes look dry and are lightly browned. Let tomatoes cool slightly; finely chop.

2. Combine tomato mixture, 3 cups reserved liquid from tomatoes, broth, tomato paste and allspice in **Crockpot™** slow cooker; stir to blend. Cover; cook on LOW 8 hours or on HIGH 4 hours.

3. Add evaporated milk and ¼ cup shredded basil; season with salt and pepper. Cover; cook on HIGH 30 minutes or until heated through. Ladle soup into bowls; garnish with additional basil.

Broccoli Cheddar Soup

makes 6 servings

3 tablespoons butter

1 medium onion, chopped

3 tablespoons all-purpose flour

¼ teaspoon ground nutmeg

¼ teaspoon black pepper

4 cups vegetable broth

1 large bunch broccoli, chopped

1 medium red potato, peeled and chopped

1 teaspoon salt

1 bay leaf

1½ cups (6 ounces) shredded Cheddar cheese, plus additional for garnish

½ cup whipping cream

1. Melt butter in medium saucepan over medium heat. Add onion; cook and stir 6 minutes or until softened. Add flour, nutmeg and pepper; cook and stir 1 minute. Remove to **Crockpot**™ slow cooker. Stir in broth, broccoli, potato, salt and bay leaf.

2. Cover; cook on HIGH 3 hours. Remove and discard bay leaf. Working in batches, place soup in food processor or blender; process until desired consistency. Pour soup back into **Crockpot**™ slow cooker. Stir in 1½ cups cheese and cream until cheese is melted. Garnish with additional cheese.

Chicken and Mushroom Stew

makes 6 servings

1 package (about 1 ounce) dried porcini mushrooms

1½ cups hot water

4 tablespoons vegetable oil, divided

2 medium leeks (white and light green parts only), halved lengthwise and thinly sliced crosswise

1 carrot, cut into 1-inch pieces

1 stalk celery, diced

6 boneless, skinless chicken thighs (about 2 pounds)

Salt and black pepper

12 ounces cremini mushrooms, quartered

¼ cup all-purpose flour

1 teaspoon minced garlic

1 fresh thyme sprig

1 bay leaf

½ cup dry white wine

1 cup chicken broth

1. To rehydrate mushrooms, place in medium bowl. Add hot water; let stand 30 minutes. Remove mushrooms with slotted spoon and coarsely chop. Strain liquid through fine-mesh strainer and reserve.

2. Heat 1 tablespoon oil in large skillet over medium heat. Add leeks; cook and stir 8 minutes or until softened. Remove to Crockpot™ slow cooker. Add carrot and celery.

3. Season chicken with salt and pepper. Heat 1 tablespoon oil in same skillet over medium-high heat. Add chicken in batches; cook 8 minutes or until browned on both sides. Remove to Crockpot™ slow cooker.

4. Heat remaining 2 tablespoons oil in same skillet. Add cremini mushrooms; cook and stir 7 minutes or until mushrooms are browned and have released their liquid. Add porcini mushrooms, flour, garlic, thyme and bay leaf; cook and stir 1 minute. Add wine; cook and stir until evaporated, scraping up browned bits from bottom of skillet. Add reserved mushroom liquid and broth; bring to a simmer. Pour mixture into Crockpot™ slow cooker.

5. Cover; cook on HIGH 2 to 3 hours. Remove and discard thyme sprig and bay leaf before serving.

Vegetable Soup with Beans

makes 6 servings

4 cups vegetable broth

1 can (about 15 ounces) cannellini beans, rinsed and drained

1 can (about 14 ounces) diced tomatoes

16 baby carrots

1 medium onion, chopped

1 ounce dried oyster mushrooms, chopped

3 tablespoons tomato paste

2 teaspoons garlic powder

1 teaspoon dried basil

1 teaspoon dried oregano

½ teaspoon salt

½ teaspoon dried rosemary

½ teaspoon dried marjoram

½ teaspoon dried sage

½ teaspoon dried thyme

¼ teaspoon black pepper

1. Combine broth, beans, tomatoes, carrots, onion, mushrooms, tomato paste, garlic powder, basil, oregano, salt, rosemary, marjoram, sage, thyme and pepper in **Crockpot**™ slow cooker; mix well.

2. Cover; cook on LOW 8 hours or on HIGH 4 hours.

Cauliflower Soup

makes 8 servings

2 heads cauliflower, cut into small florets

8 cups vegetable or chicken broth

¾ cup chopped celery

¾ cup chopped onion

2 teaspoons salt

2 teaspoons black pepper

2 cups milk or whipping cream

1 teaspoon Worcestershire sauce

1. Combine cauliflower, broth, celery, onion, salt and pepper in **Crockpot**™ slow cooker. Cover; cook on LOW 7 to 8 hours or on HIGH 3 to 4 hours.

2. Working in batches, place soup in food processor or blender; process until smooth. Add milk and Worcestershire sauce; process until blended. Pour soup back into **Crockpot**™ slow cooker. Cover; cook on HIGH 15 to 20 minutes or until heated through.

Lamb and Chickpea Stew

makes 6 servings

1 pound lamb stew meat

2 teaspoons salt, divided

2 tablespoons vegetable oil, divided

1 large onion, chopped

1 tablespoon minced garlic

1½ teaspoons ground cumin

1 teaspoon ground turmeric

1 teaspoon ground coriander

1 teaspoon ground cinnamon

¼ teaspoon black pepper

2 cups chicken broth

1 cup diced canned tomatoes, drained

1 cup dried chickpeas, rinsed and sorted

½ cup chopped dried apricots

¼ cup chopped fresh parsley

2 tablespoons honey

2 tablespoons lemon juice

Hot cooked couscous

1. Season lamb with 1 teaspoon salt. Heat 1 tablespoon oil in large skillet over medium-high heat. Add lamb; cook and stir 8 minutes or until browned on all sides. Remove to **Crockpot**™ slow cooker.

2. Heat remaining 1 tablespoon oil in same skillet over medium heat. Add onion; cook and stir 6 minutes or until softened. Add garlic, remaining 1 teaspoon salt, cumin, turmeric, coriander, cinnamon and pepper; cook and stir 1 minute. Add broth and tomatoes; cook and stir 5 minutes, scraping up any browned bits from bottom of skillet. Remove to **Crockpot**™ slow cooker. Stir in chickpeas.

3. Cover; cook on LOW 7 hours. Stir in apricots. Cover; cook on LOW 1 hour. Turn off heat. Let stand 10 minutes. Skim off and discard fat. Stir in parsley, honey and lemon juice. Serve over couscous.

French Onion Soup

makes 8 servings

¼ **cup (½ stick) butter**
3 **pounds yellow onions, sliced**
1 **tablespoon sugar**
3 **tablespoons dry white wine or water**
8 **cups beef broth**
8 **to 16 slices French bread**
1 **cup (4 ounces) shredded Gruyère or Swiss cheese**

1. Melt butter in large skillet over medium-low heat. Add onions; cover and cook 10 minutes or just until onions are tender and transparent, but not browned.

2. Remove cover. Sprinkle sugar over onions; cook and stir 15 minutes or until onions are lightly browned. Add onions to **Crockpot**™ slow cooker. Add wine, scraping up any browned bits from bottom of skillet. Add to **Crockpot**™ slow cooker. Stir in broth. Cover; cook on LOW 8 hours or on HIGH 6 hours.

3. To serve, preheat broiler. Ladle soup into individual ovenproof soup bowls; place on baking sheet. Top each serving with one or two bread slices and cheese. Place under broiler until cheese is melted and bubbly.

Variation: Substitute 1 cup dry white wine for 1 cup of the broth.

Chuck and Stout Soup

makes 6 to 8 servings

8 cups beef broth

3 pounds boneless beef chuck roast, cut into 1-inch cubes

Salt and black pepper

2 tablespoons olive oil

3 onions, thinly sliced

6 carrots, diced

3 stalks celery, diced

4 cloves garlic, minced

2 packages (10 ounces *each*) cremini mushrooms, thinly sliced

1 package (about 1 ounce) dried porcini mushrooms, processed to a fine powder*

4 fresh thyme sprigs

1 can (12 ounces) Irish stout

To turn the mushrooms into a powder, use a coffee grinder, food processor or blender.

1. Bring broth to a boil in large saucepan over high heat. Reduce heat to low; simmer until reduced by half.

2. Meanwhile, season beef with salt and pepper. Heat oil in large skillet over medium-high heat. Add beef in batches; cook 5 to 7 minutes or until browned on all sides, turning occasionally. Remove beef to **Crockpot**™ slow cooker.

3. Add reduced broth, onions, carrots, celery, garlic, cremini mushrooms, mushroom powder, thyme and stout to **Crockpot**™ slow cooker. Cover; cook on LOW 10 hours or on HIGH 6 hours. Remove and discard thyme sprigs.

Chilies

Turkey Chili

makes 6 servings

2 tablespoons olive oil, divided

1½ pounds ground turkey

2 medium onions, chopped

1 medium red bell pepper, chopped

1 medium green bell pepper, chopped

5 cloves garlic, minced

1 jalapeño pepper, finely chopped*

2 cans (about 14 ounces *each*) fire-roasted diced tomatoes

4 teaspoons chili powder

1 teaspoon ground cumin

1 teaspoon dried oregano

½ teaspoon salt

Jalapeño peppers can sting and irritate the skin, so wear rubber gloves when handling peppers and do not touch your eyes.

1. Heat 1 tablespoon oil in large skillet over medium-high heat. Add turkey; cook 7 minutes or until no longer pink, stirring to break up meat. Remove to **Crockpot**™ slow cooker using slotted spoon. Drain any liquid remaining in skillet.

2. Heat remaining 1 tablespoon oil in same skillet over medium-high heat. Add onions, bell peppers, garlic and jalapeño pepper; cook and stir 4 to 5 minutes or until softened. Stir in tomatoes, chili powder, cumin, oregano and salt; cook and stir 1 minute. Stir vegetable mixture into turkey in **Crockpot**™ slow cooker; mix well. Cover; cook on LOW 6 hours.

Beef and Black Bean Chili

makes 4 servings

1 tablespoon vegetable oil

1 pound boneless beef round steak, cut into 1-inch cubes

1 package (14 ounces) frozen bell pepper strips with onions

1 can (about 15 ounces) black beans, rinsed and drained

1 can (about 14 ounces) fire-roasted diced tomatoes

2 tablespoons chili powder

1 tablespoon minced garlic

2 teaspoons ground cumin

1 teaspoon salt

½ ounce semisweet chocolate, chopped

Hot cooked rice

Shredded Cheddar cheese (optional)

1. Heat oil in large skillet over medium-high heat. Add beef; cook 6 to 8 minutes or until browned on all sides, turning occasionally. Remove to **Crockpot**™ slow cooker using slotted spoon.

2. Stir pepper strips with onions, beans, tomatoes, chili powder, garlic, cumin and salt into **Crockpot**™ slow cooker. Cover; cook on LOW 8 to 9 hours. Turn off heat; stir in chocolate until melted. Serve over rice; garnish with cheese.

Hearty Pork and Bacon Chili

makes 8 to 10 servings

2½ pounds boneless pork shoulder, cut into 1-inch pieces

3½ teaspoons salt, divided

1¼ teaspoons black pepper, divided

1 tablespoon vegetable oil

4 slices thick-cut bacon, diced

2 medium onions, chopped

1 red bell pepper, chopped

¼ cup chili powder

2 tablespoons tomato paste

1 tablespoon minced garlic

1 tablespoon ground cumin

1 tablespoon smoked paprika

1 bottle (12 ounces) pale ale

2 cans (about 14 ounces *each*) diced tomatoes

2 cups water

¾ cup dried kidney beans, rinsed and sorted

¾ cup dried black beans, rinsed and sorted

3 tablespoons cornmeal

Crumbled queso fresco or feta cheese and chopped fresh cilantro (optional)

1. Season pork with 1 teaspoon salt and 1 teaspoon black pepper. Heat oil in large skillet over medium-high heat. Add pork in batches; cook 6 minutes or until browned on all sides, turning occasionally. Remove to **Crockpot**™ slow cooker using slotted spoon.

2. Heat same skillet over medium heat. Add bacon; cook and stir until crisp. Remove to **Crockpot**™ slow cooker using slotted spoon.

3. Pour off all but 2 tablespoons drippings from skillet. Heat skillet over medium heat. Add onions and bell pepper; cook and stir 6 minutes or until softened. Stir in chili powder, tomato paste, garlic, cumin, paprika, remaining 2½ teaspoons salt and remaining ¼ teaspoon black pepper; cook and stir 1 minute. Stir in ale. Bring to a simmer, scraping up any browned bits from bottom of skillet. Pour over pork in **Crockpot**™ slow cooker. Stir in tomatoes, water, beans and cornmeal.

4. Cover; cook on LOW 10 hours. Turn off heat; let stand 10 minutes. Skim fat from surface. Garnish each serving with cheese and cilantro.

Texas Chili

makes 8 servings

3½ to 4 pounds cubed beef stew meat

Salt and black pepper

4 tablespoons vegetable oil, divided

1 large onion, diced

¼ cup chili powder

1 tablespoon minced garlic

1 tablespoon tomato paste

1 tablespoon ground cumin

2 teaspoons ground coriander

1 teaspoon dried oregano

3 cans (about 14 ounces *each*) diced tomatoes

3 tablespoons cornmeal or masa harina

1 tablespoon packed brown sugar

1. Season beef with salt and pepper. Heat 3 tablespoons oil in large skillet over medium-high heat. Cook beef in batches 8 minutes or until browned on all sides, turning occasionally. Remove to **Crockpot**™ slow cooker using slotted spoon.

2. Heat remaining 1 tablespoon oil in same skillet. Add onion; cook and stir 6 minutes or until softened. Stir in chili powder, garlic, tomato paste, cumin, coriander, oregano and additional salt and pepper as desired; cook and stir 1 minute. Stir in tomatoes, cornmeal and brown sugar; bring to a simmer. Remove to **Crockpot**™ slow cooker. Cover; cook on LOW 7 to 8 hours.

Variation: Add ¼ teaspoon ground red pepper for spicier chili.

Three-Bean Chili with Chorizo

makes 6 to 8 servings

2 Mexican chorizo sausages (about 6 ounces *each*), casings removed

1 tablespoon vegetable oil

1 large onion, chopped

1 tablespoon salt

1 tablespoon tomato paste

1 tablespoon minced garlic

1 tablespoon chili powder

1 tablespoon ancho chili powder

2 to 3 teaspoons chipotle chili powder

2 teaspoons ground cumin

1 teaspoon ground coriander

3 cups water

2 cans (about 14 ounces *each*) crushed tomatoes

½ cup dried pinto beans, rinsed and sorted

½ cup dried kidney beans, rinsed and sorted

½ cup dried black beans, rinsed and sorted

Chopped fresh cilantro (optional)

1. Heat large nonstick skillet over medium-high heat. Add sausages; cook 3 to 4 minutes, stirring to break up meat. Remove to **Crockpot**™ slow cooker using slotted spoon.

2. Wipe out skillet. Heat oil in same skillet over medium heat. Add onion; cook and stir 6 minutes or until softened. Add salt, tomato paste, garlic, chili powders, cumin and coriander; cook and stir 1 minute. Remove to **Crockpot**™ slow cooker. Stir in water, tomatoes and beans. Cover; cook on LOW 10 hours. Garnish each serving with cilantro.

Note: For spicier chili, increase chipotle chili powder to 1 tablespoon.

Bean and Corn Chili

makes 6 servings

1 tablespoon olive oil

2 medium onions, finely chopped

5 cloves garlic, minced

2 tablespoons dry red wine

2 cans (about 15 ounces *each*) kidney beans, rinsed and drained

6 plum tomatoes, chopped

1½ cups vegetable broth

1 green bell pepper, finely chopped

1 red bell pepper, finely chopped

1 cup frozen corn

1 stalk celery, finely sliced

1 can (6 ounces) tomato paste

1 teaspoon salt

1 teaspoon chili powder

½ teaspoon black pepper

¼ teaspoon ground cumin

¼ teaspoon dried oregano

¼ teaspoon ground coriander

¼ teaspoon ground red pepper

1. Heat oil in medium skillet over medium-high heat. Add onions, garlic and red wine; cook and stir until onions are tender. Remove to **Crockpot**™ slow cooker.

2. Stir beans, tomatoes, broth, bell peppers, corn, celery, tomato paste, salt, chili powder, black pepper, cumin, oregano, coriander and ground red pepper into **Crockpot**™ slow cooker; mix well. Cover; cook on LOW 6 to 8 hours or on HIGH 3 to 4 hours.

Tip: This recipe can be doubled for a 5-, 6- or 7-quart **Crockpot**™ slow cooker.

Simple Beef Chili

makes 8 servings

3 **pounds ground beef**

2 **cans (about 14 ounces *each*) diced tomatoes**

2 **cans (about 15 ounces *each*) kidney beans, rinsed and drained**

2 **cups chopped onions**

1 **package (10 ounces) frozen corn**

1 **cup chopped green bell pepper**

1 **can (8 ounces) tomato sauce**

3 **tablespoons chili powder**

2 **teaspoons salt**

1 **teaspoon garlic powder**

½ **teaspoon ground cumin**

½ **teaspoon dried oregano**

1. Brown beef in large skillet over medium-high heat 6 to 8 minutes, stirring to break up meat. Remove to **Crockpot**™ slow cooker using slotted spoon.

2. Stir tomatoes, beans, onions, corn, bell pepper, tomato sauce, chili powder, salt, garlic powder, cumin and oregano into **Crockpot**™ slow cooker; mix well. Cover; cook on LOW 4 hours.

Tip: The flavor and aroma of crushed or ground herbs and spices may lessen during a longer cooking time. So, when slow cooking in your **Crockpot**™ slow cooker, be sure to taste and adjust seasonings, if necessary, before serving.

Chicken Chili

makes 4 to 6 servings

1 tablespoon vegetable oil

1½ pounds boneless, skinless chicken thighs, cut into 1-inch pieces

1 large onion, chopped

1 medium red bell pepper, chopped

1 medium green bell pepper, chopped

4 cloves garlic, minced

2 cans (about 14 ounces *each*) diced tomatoes with mild green chiles

1 can (6 ounces) tomato paste

1 can (about 15 ounces) small white beans, rinsed and drained

1 can (about 8¾ ounces) corn, drained

1½ tablespoons chili powder

1 teaspoon salt

Optional toppings: shredded Cheddar cheese, sliced fresh chives and/or sour cream

1. Coat inside of **Crockpot**™ slow cooker with nonstick cooking spray. Heat oil in large skillet over medium-high heat. Add chicken; cook and stir 5 to 6 minutes until lightly browned, turning occasionally. Remove chicken to **Crockpot**™ slow cooker.

2. Add onion, bell peppers and garlic to same skillet; cook and stir 5 minutes or until softened. Remove onion mixture to **Crockpot**™ slow cooker. Stir in tomatoes, tomato paste, beans, corn, chili powder and salt. Cover; cook on LOW 7 to 8 hours or on HIGH 3 to 4 hours. Serve with desired toppings.

Main Meats

Easy Salisbury Steak

makes 4 servings

1 medium onion, sliced

1½ pounds ground beef

1 egg

½ cup seasoned dry bread crumbs

2 teaspoons Worcestershire sauce, divided

1 teaspoon ground mustard

1 can (10½ ounces) cream of mushroom soup

½ cup water

3 tablespoons ketchup

½ cup sliced mushrooms

Chopped fresh parsley (optional)

1. Coat inside of **Crockpot**™ slow cooker with nonstick cooking spray. Spread onion on bottom of **Crockpot**™ slow cooker.

2. Combine beef, egg, bread crumbs, 1 teaspoon Worcestershire sauce and mustard in large bowl. Shape into four 1-inch-thick oval patties.

3. Heat large nonstick skillet over medium-high heat. Add patties; cook 2 minutes per side or until lightly browned. Remove to **Crockpot**™ slow cooker. Stir soup, water, ketchup and remaining 1 teaspoon Worcestershire sauce in medium bowl. Pour mixture over patties; top with mushrooms. Cover; cook on LOW 3 to 3½ hours. Garnish with parsley.

Serving Suggestion: Serve with mashed potatoes and steamed peas.

Pineapple and Pork Teriyaki

makes 6 to 8 servings

1 tablespoon vegetable oil

2 pork tenderloins (1¼ pounds *each*)

1 can (8 ounces) pineapple chunks

½ cup teriyaki sauce

3 tablespoons honey

1 tablespoon minced fresh ginger

2 teaspoons cold water

1 teaspoon cornstarch

1. Heat oil in large skillet over medium-high heat. Add pork; cook 8 minutes or until browned on all sides. Remove to **Crockpot**™ slow cooker.

2. Combine pineapple with juice, teriyaki sauce, honey and ginger in large bowl; stir to blend. Pour over pork. Cover; cook on LOW 6 to 7 hours or on HIGH 3 to 4 hours. Remove pork to large cutting board; cover loosely with foil. Let stand 15 minutes before slicing.

3. Stir water into cornstarch in small bowl until smooth. Stir into liquid in **Crockpot**™ slow cooker. Cook, uncovered, on HIGH 10 to 15 minutes or until sauce is thickened. Serve sliced pork with pineapple and cooking liquid.

Pot Roast with Bacon and Mushrooms

makes 6 servings

6 slices bacon

1 boneless beef chuck roast (2½ to 3 pounds), trimmed*

¾ teaspoon salt, divided

¼ teaspoon black pepper

¾ cup chopped shallots

8 ounces sliced white mushrooms

¼ ounce dried porcini mushrooms (optional)

4 cloves garlic, minced

1 teaspoon dried oregano

1 cup beef broth

2 tablespoons tomato paste

Roasted Cauliflower (recipe follows, optional)

Unless you have a 5-, 6- or 7-quart Crockpot™ slow cooker, cut any roast larger than 2½ pounds in half so it cooks completely.

1. Heat large skillet over medium heat. Add bacon; cook and stir until crisp. Remove to paper towel-lined plate using tongs; crumble when cool enough to handle.

2. Pour off all but 2 tablespoons drippings from skillet. Season roast with ½ teaspoon salt and pepper. Heat same skillet over medium-high heat. Add roast; cook 8 minutes or until well browned. Remove to large plate. Add shallots, white mushrooms, porcini mushrooms, if desired, garlic, oregano and remaining ¼ teaspoon salt; cook 3 to 4 minutes or until shallots are softened. Remove shallot mixture to **Crockpot**™ slow cooker.

3. Stir bacon into **Crockpot**™ slow cooker. Place roast on top of vegetables. Whisk broth and tomato paste in small bowl until well blended. Pour broth mixture over roast. Cover; cook on LOW 8 hours.

4. Prepare Roasted Cauliflower, if desired. Remove roast to large cutting board. Let stand 10 minutes before slicing. Serve with vegetables, cooking liquid and Roasted Cauliflower.

Roasted Cauliflower: Preheat oven to 375°F. Cut one head of cauliflower into florets; spread on large baking sheet. Drizzle with olive oil and season with salt and pepper; toss to coat. Roast 20 minutes. Turn; roast 15 minutes.

Boneless Pork Roast with Garlic

makes 4 to 6 servings

1 boneless pork rib roast (2 to 2½ pounds)

Salt and black pepper

3 tablespoons olive oil, divided

4 cloves garlic, minced

¼ cup chopped fresh rosemary

½ lemon, cut into ⅛- to ¼-inch slices

½ cup chicken broth

¼ cup dry white wine

1. Season pork all over with salt and pepper. Combine 2 tablespoons oil, garlic and rosemary in small bowl. Rub over pork. Roll and tie pork with kitchen string. Tuck lemon slices under string and into ends of roast.

2. Heat remaining 1 tablespoon oil in large skillet over medium heat. Add pork; cook 6 to 8 minutes or until browned on all sides. Remove to **Crockpot**™ slow cooker.

3. Return skillet to heat. Add broth and wine, scraping up any browned bits from bottom of skillet. Pour over pork in **Crockpot**™ slow cooker. Cover; cook on LOW 8 to 9 hours or on HIGH 3 to 4 hours.

4. Remove roast to large cutting board. Cover loosely with foil; let stand 10 to 15 minutes before removing kitchen string and slicing. Pour pan juices over sliced pork to serve.

Mexican Carnitas

makes 4 servings

1 boneless pork shoulder roast (2 pounds), cut into 2-inch pieces
1 tablespoon garlic salt
1 tablespoon black pepper
1½ teaspoons adobo seasoning
1 medium onion, chopped
1 can (16 ounces) green salsa
½ cup water
¼ cup chopped fresh cilantro
  Juice of 2 limes
3 cloves garlic, minced
4 (6-inch) flour tortillas, warmed
  Optional toppings: chopped green bell pepper, tomatoes and red onion

1. Coat inside of **Crockpot**™ slow cooker with nonstick cooking spray. Season pork with garlic salt, black pepper and adobo seasoning.

2. Place pork, onion, salsa, water, cilantro, lime juice and garlic in **Crockpot**™ slow cooker. Cover; cook on LOW 4 to 5 hours or until pork is tender.

3. Remove pork to medium bowl; shred with two forks. Stir back into sauce in **Crockpot**™ slow cooker. Serve pork in tortillas with desired toppings.

Molasses Maple-Glazed Beef Brisket

makes 4 to 6 servings

1 beef brisket (about 3 pounds), cut in half and scored on both sides

4 slices (1/16 inch thick) fresh ginger

4 slices (1/2 inch×1 1/2 inches) orange peel

1/2 cup maple syrup

1/4 cup molasses

Juice of 1 orange

2 tablespoons packed brown sugar

2 tablespoons olive oil

1 tablespoon tomato paste

2 cloves garlic, minced

1 tablespoon salt

1 teaspoon ground red pepper

1/2 teaspoon black pepper

1. Combine brisket, ginger, orange peel, syrup, molasses, orange juice, brown sugar, oil, tomato paste, garlic, salt, ground red pepper and black pepper in large resealable food storage bag. Seal bag; turn to coat. Refrigerate 2 hours or overnight, turning bag several times.

2. Remove brisket and marinade to **Crockpot**™ slow cooker. Cover; cook on LOW 7 to 9 hours or on HIGH 3 1/2 to 4 hours. Remove brisket to large cutting board; thinly slice across grain.

Serving Suggestion: Serve with mashed potatoes and steamed green beans.

Classic Pot Roast
makes 6 to 8 servings

1 boneless beef chuck roast
  (3 to 4 pounds)*

Salt and black pepper

1 tablespoon vegetable oil

6 medium potatoes, cut into
  halves

6 carrots, cut into 2-inch pieces

2 medium onions, cut into
  quarters

2 stalks celery, sliced

1 can (about 14 ounces) diced
  tomatoes

Dried oregano

2 tablespoons water

2 tablespoons all-purpose flour

*Unless you have a 5-, 6- or 7-quart
Crockpot™ slow cooker, cut any roast
larger than 2½ pounds in half so it
cooks completely.*

1. Season roast all over with salt and pepper. Heat oil in large skillet over medium-low heat. Add roast; cook 6 to 8 minutes or until browned on all sides. Remove to **Crockpot**™ slow cooker.

2. Add potatoes, carrots, onions, celery, tomatoes, salt, pepper, oregano and enough water to cover bottom of **Crockpot**™ slow cooker by about ½ inch. Cover; cook on LOW 8 to 10 hours.

3. Turn off heat. Remove roast and vegetables to large serving platter using slotted spoon. Let cooking liquid stand 5 minutes. Skim off fat and discard.

4. Turn **Crockpot**™ slow cooker to HIGH. Stir 2 tablespoons water into flour in small bowl until smooth; whisk into cooking liquid. Cover; cook on HIGH 10 to 15 minutes or until thickened. Serve sauce over roast and vegetables.

Bacon, Onion and Stout Braised Short Ribs

makes 4 to 6 servings

4 pounds bone-in beef short ribs, well trimmed

1 teaspoon salt, plus additional for seasoning

½ teaspoon black pepper, plus additional for seasoning

1 tablespoon vegetable oil

6 ounces thick-cut bacon, cut into ¼-inch slices

1 large onion, halved and cut into ¼-inch slices

2 tablespoons all-purpose flour

2 tablespoons spicy brown mustard

1 tablespoon tomato paste

1 can (12 ounces) Irish stout

1 cup beef broth

1 bay leaf

2 tablespoons finely chopped fresh parsley

1. Season beef with salt and pepper. Heat oil in large skillet over medium-high heat until almost smoking. Add short ribs in batches; cook 5 to 7 minutes or until browned on all sides. Remove to **Crockpot**™ slow cooker.

2. Wipe out skillet with paper towels. Heat same skillet over medium heat. Add bacon; cook and stir until crisp. Remove to paper towel-lined plate using slotted spoon. Remove and discard all but 1 tablespoon drippings from skillet.

3. Heat skillet over medium heat. Add onion; cook and stir 5 minutes or until softened and translucent. Add flour, mustard, tomato paste, 1 teaspoon salt and ½ teaspoon pepper; cook 1 minute, stirring constantly. Remove skillet from heat and pour in stout, stirring to scrape up any browned bits from bottom of skillet. Pour stout mixture over ribs. Add bacon, broth and bay leaf to **Crockpot**™ slow cooker. Cover; cook on LOW 8 hours.

4. Turn off heat. Remove beef to large serving platter. Let cooking liquid stand 5 minutes. Skim off and discard fat. Remove and discard bay leaf. Stir in parsley.

Serving Suggestion: Serve with mashed potatoes or buttered egg noodles.

Pork Roast with Fruit Medley

makes 6 to 8 servings

1 cup water

½ cup salt

2 tablespoons sugar

1 teaspoon dried thyme

2 bay leaves

1 boneless pork loin roast (about 4 pounds), trimmed*

2 tablespoons vegetable oil

2 cups green grapes

1 cup dried apricots

1 cup dried prunes

1 cup dry red wine

2 cloves garlic, minced

Juice of ½ lemon

Unless you have a 5-, 6- or 7-quart Crockpot™ slow cooker, cut any roast larger than 2½ pounds in half so it cooks completely.

1. Combine water, salt, sugar, thyme and bay leaves in large resealable food storage bag; add roast. Seal bag; turn to coat. Marinate overnight or up to 2 days in refrigerator, turning occasionally.

2. Remove roast from marinade; lightly pat dry. Heat oil in large skillet over medium heat. Add roast; cook 8 to 10 minutes or until browned on all sides. Remove to **Crockpot**™ slow cooker.

3. Add grapes, apricots, prunes, wine, garlic and lemon juice; stir to blend. Cover; cook on LOW 7 to 9 hours or on HIGH 3 to 5 hours.

4. Remove pork to cutting board; let stand 10 minutes before slicing. Serve with fruit.

Southern Smothered Pork Chops

makes 6 to 8 servings

6 to 8 bone-in pork chops
  Salt and black pepper
2 tablespoons vegetable oil
3 cups water
1 can (10½ ounces) cream of
  mushroom soup
1 large onion, chopped
5 cloves garlic, chopped
2 tablespoons Italian seasoning
1 package (about ½ ounce) pork
  gravy mix
1 package (about 1 ounce)
  dry mushroom and onion
  soup mix

1. Season pork with salt and pepper. Heat oil in large skillet over medium-high heat. Add pork; brown 3 to 4 minutes on each side.

2. Place water, soup, onion, garlic, Italian seasoning, gravy mix and dry soup mix in **Crockpot**™ slow cooker; stir to blend. Add pork; turn to coat. Cover; cook on LOW 5 hours.

Serving Suggestion: Serve with steamed corn on the cob.

Corned Beef and Cabbage

makes 6 servings

2 onions, thickly sliced

1 corned beef brisket with seasoning packet (about 3 pounds)

1 package (8 to 10 ounces) baby carrots

6 medium potatoes, cut into wedges

1 cup water

3 to 5 slices bacon

1 head green cabbage, cut into wedges

1. Place onions in bottom of **Crockpot**™ slow cooker. Add corned beef with seasoning packet, carrots and potato wedges. Pour 1 cup water over top. Cover; cook on LOW 10 hours.

2. With 30 minutes left in cooking time, heat large saucepan over medium heat. Add bacon; cook and stir until crisp. Remove to paper towel-lined plate using tongs. Reserve drippings in saucepan. Crumble bacon when cool enough to handle.

3. Place cabbage in saucepan with bacon drippings; add water to cover. Bring to a boil; cook 20 to 30 minutes or until cabbage is tender. Drain. Remove corned beef to cutting board. Cut into slices. Serve with vegetables.

Braised Lamb Shanks

makes 4 servings

4 lamb shanks (12 to 14 ounces *each*)

¾ teaspoon salt, divided

¼ teaspoon black pepper

1 tablespoon olive oil

1 medium onion, chopped

2 stalks celery, chopped

2 carrots, chopped

6 cloves garlic, minced

1 teaspoon dried basil

1 can (about 14 ounces) diced tomatoes

2 tablespoons tomato paste

Chopped fresh parsley (optional)

1. Coat inside of **Crockpot**™ slow cooker with nonstick cooking spray. Season lamb with ½ teaspoon salt and pepper. Heat oil in large skillet over medium-high heat. Add lamb; cook 8 to 10 minutes or until browned on all sides. Remove lamb to **Crockpot**™ slow cooker.

2. Return skillet to medium-high heat. Add onion, celery, carrots, garlic and basil; cook and stir 3 to 4 minutes or until vegetables are softened. Add tomatoes, tomato paste and remaining ¼ teaspoon salt; cook and stir 2 to 3 minutes or until slightly thickened. Pour tomato mixture over lamb shanks in **Crockpot**™ slow cooker.

3. Cover; cook on LOW 8 to 9 hours or until lamb is very tender. Remove lamb to large serving platter; cover to keep warm. Turn **Crockpot**™ slow cooker to HIGH. Cook, uncovered, on HIGH 10 to 15 minutes or until sauce is thickened. Serve lamb with sauce. Garnish with parsley.

Beef and Veal Meat Loaf

makes 6 servings

1 tablespoon olive oil
1 small onion, chopped
½ red bell pepper, chopped
3 cloves garlic, minced
1 teaspoon dried oregano
1 pound ground beef
1 pound ground veal
1 egg
3 tablespoons tomato paste
1 teaspoon salt
½ teaspoon black pepper

1. Coat inside of **Crockpot**™ slow cooker with nonstick cooking spray. Heat oil in large skillet over medium-high heat. Add onion, bell pepper, garlic and oregano; cook and stir 5 minutes or until vegetables are softened. Remove onion mixture to large bowl; cool 5 minutes.

2. Add beef, veal, egg, tomato paste, salt and black pepper to onion mixture; mix well. Shape into 9×5-inch loaf; place in **Crockpot**™ slow cooker.

3. Cover; cook on LOW 5 to 6 hours. Remove meat loaf to cutting board; let stand 10 minutes before slicing.

Poultry & Fish

Caribbean Jerk Chicken

makes 6 servings

6 boneless, skinless chicken thighs

1 small yellow onion

¼ cup chicken broth

¼ cup soy sauce

1 large jalapeño pepper, stemmed and seeded*

2 teaspoons minced garlic

1 teaspoon ground ginger

1 teaspoon dried thyme

¼ teaspoon ground cloves

⅛ teaspoon ground allspice

⅛ teaspoon ground cinnamon

Jalapeño peppers can sting and irritate the skin, so wear rubber gloves when handling peppers and do not touch your eyes.

1. Coat inside of **Crockpot**™ slow cooker with nonstick cooking spray; add chicken.

2. Combine onion, broth, soy sauce, jalapeño pepper, garlic, ginger, thyme, cloves, allspice and cinnamon in food processor or blender; process until well blended. Pour onion mixture over chicken in **Crockpot**™ slow cooker.

3. Cover; cook on HIGH 3 hours.

Serving Suggestion: Serve with frozen cauliflower rice, prepared according to package directions, or hot cooked rice.

Raspberry BBQ Chicken Wings

makes 5 to 6 servings

3 pounds chicken drummettes and wings, tips removed and split at joints

¾ cup seedless raspberry jam

½ cup sweet and tangy prepared barbecue sauce

1 tablespoon raspberry red wine vinegar

1 teaspoon chili powder

1. Coat inside of **Crockpot**™ slow cooker with nonstick cooking spray. Preheat broiler. Spray large baking sheet with cooking spray. Arrange chicken on prepared baking sheet. Broil 6 to 8 minutes or until browned, turning once. Remove to **Crockpot**™ slow cooker.

2. Combine jam, barbecue sauce, vinegar and chili powder in medium bowl; stir to blend. Pour sauce over chicken in **Crockpot**™ slow cooker; turn to coat. Cover; cook on LOW 3½ to 4 hours. Remove chicken to large serving platter; cover to keep warm.

3. Turn **Crockpot**™ slow cooker to HIGH. Cook, uncovered, on HIGH 10 to 15 minutes or until sauce is thickened. Spoon sauce over chicken to serve.

Miso-Poached Salmon

makes 6 servings

1½ cups water

2 green onions, cut into 2-inch
   long pieces

¼ cup yellow miso paste

¼ cup soy sauce

2 tablespoons sake

2 tablespoons mirin

1½ teaspoons grated fresh ginger

1 teaspoon minced garlic

6 salmon fillets (4 ounces *each*)

   Hot cooked rice

   Thinly sliced green onions
      (optional)

1. Combine water, 2 green onions, miso paste, soy sauce, sake, mirin, ginger and garlic in **Crockpot**™ slow cooker; stir to blend. Cover; cook on HIGH 30 minutes.

2. Turn **Crockpot**™ slow cooker to LOW. Add salmon, skin side down. Cover; cook on LOW 30 minutes to 1 hour or until salmon turns opaque and flakes easily with fork.

3. Serve salmon over rice drizzled with cooking liquid, if desired. Garnish with sliced green onions.

Shrimp Jambalaya

makes 8 servings

1 package (8 ounces) New Orleans style jambalaya mix

2½ cups chicken broth

1 can (about 14 ounces) diced tomatoes with green pepper, celery and onion

8 ounces andouille sausage, cut into ¼-inch-thick slices

1 teaspoon hot pepper sauce, plus additional for serving

1½ pounds large raw shrimp, peeled and deveined (with tails on)

1. Coat inside of **Crockpot**™ slow cooker with nonstick cooking spray. Add jambalaya mix, broth, tomatoes, sausage and 1 teaspoon hot pepper sauce; stir to blend. Cover; cook on LOW 2½ to 3 hours or until rice is cooked through.

2. Stir in shrimp. Cover; cook on LOW 30 minutes or until shrimp are cooked through. Serve with additional hot pepper sauce.

Coconut-Curry Chicken Thighs

makes 4 servings

8 chicken boneless, skinless thighs (about 2 to 2½ pounds)
½ teaspoon salt
¼ teaspoon black pepper
1 tablespoon olive oil
1 medium onion, chopped
1 medium red bell pepper, chopped
3 cloves garlic, minced
1 tablespoon grated fresh ginger
1 can (about 13 ounces) unsweetened coconut milk
3 tablespoons honey
1 tablespoon Thai red curry paste
2 teaspoons Thai roasted red chili paste
2 tablespoons chopped fresh cilantro (optional)
½ cup chopped cashew nuts (optional)

1. Coat inside of **Crockpot**™ slow cooker with nonstick cooking spray. Season chicken with salt and black pepper. Heat oil in large skillet over medium-high heat. Add chicken; cook 6 to 8 minutes or until browned on both sides. Remove to **Crockpot**™ slow cooker.

2. Pour off all but 1 tablespoon drippings from skillet. Heat skillet over medium-high heat. Add onion, bell pepper, garlic and ginger; cook and stir 3 minutes or until vegetables begin to soften. Remove skillet from heat. Stir in coconut milk, honey, curry paste and chili paste until smooth. Pour coconut mixture over chicken in **Crockpot**™ slow cooker.

3. Cover; cook on LOW 4 hours. Serve chicken with sauce, cilantro and cashews, if desired.

Slow Cooker Chicken Dinner

makes 4 servings

1 can (10½ ounces) condensed cream of chicken soup, undiluted

⅓ cup milk

4 boneless, skinless chicken breasts (about 2 pounds)

1 package (6 ounces) stuffing mix

1⅔ cups water

1. Combine soup and milk in **Crockpot**™ slow cooker; stir to blend. Add chicken.

2. Combine stuffing mix and water in large bowl; stir to blend. Spoon stuffing over chicken. Cover; cook on LOW 6 to 8 hours.

Boneless Chicken Cacciatore

makes 6 servings

1 tablespoon olive oil

6 boneless, skinless chicken breasts, sliced in half horizontally

4 cups tomato-basil pasta sauce

1 cup chopped yellow onion

1 cup chopped green bell pepper

1 can (6 ounces) sliced mushrooms, drained

¼ cup dry red wine

2 teaspoons minced garlic

2 teaspoons dried oregano

2 teaspoons dried thyme

2 teaspoons salt

2 teaspoons black pepper

Hot cooked pasta

1. Heat oil in large skillet over medium heat. Add chicken; cook 6 to 8 minutes or until browned on both sides. Remove to **Crockpot**™ slow cooker using slotted spoon.

2. Add pasta sauce, onion, bell pepper, mushrooms, wine, garlic, oregano, thyme, salt and black pepper to **Crockpot**™ slow cooker; mix well. Cover; cook on LOW 4 hours or on HIGH 2 hours. Serve chicken and sauce over pasta.

Chicken Provençal

makes 8 servings

3½ **pounds boneless, skinless chicken thighs, cut into halves**

1 **medium red bell pepper, cut into ¼-inch-thick slices**

1 **medium yellow bell pepper, cut into ¼-inch-thick slices**

1 **medium onion, thinly sliced**

1 **can (28 ounces) plum tomatoes, drained**

¼ **cup chicken broth**

3 **cloves garlic, minced**

¼ **teaspoon salt**

¼ **teaspoon dried thyme**

¼ **teaspoon ground fennel seed**

3 **strips orange peel**

½ **cup chopped fresh basil**

Combine chicken, bell peppers, onion, tomatoes, broth, garlic, salt, thyme, fennel seed and orange peel in **Crockpot**™ slow cooker; mix well. Cover; cook on LOW 6 to 8 hours or on HIGH 3 to 4 hours. Sprinkle with basil just before serving.

Note: This recipe can be doubled for a 5-, 6- or 7-quart **Crockpot**™ slow cooker.

Chicken Meatballs in Spicy Tomato Sauce

makes 4 servings

3 tablespoons olive oil, divided
1 medium onion, chopped
6 cloves garlic, minced
1½ teaspoons dried basil
¼ teaspoon red pepper flakes
2 cans (about 14 ounces *each*) diced tomatoes
3 tablespoons tomato paste
2 teaspoons salt, divided
1½ pounds ground chicken
2 egg yolks
1 teaspoon dried oregano
¼ teaspoon black pepper

1. Heat 2 tablespoons oil in large skillet over medium-high heat. Add onion, garlic, basil and red pepper flakes; cook and stir 5 minutes or until onion is softened. Remove half of mixture to **Crockpot**™ slow cooker; stir in diced tomatoes, tomato paste and 1 teaspoon salt.

2. Remove remaining onion mixture to large bowl. Add chicken, egg yolks, oregano, remaining 1 teaspoon salt and black pepper; mix well. Shape mixture into 24 (1-inch) balls.

3. Heat remaining 1 tablespoon oil in large skillet. Add meatballs in batches; cook 7 minutes or until browned. Remove to **Crockpot**™ slow cooker using slotted spoon. Cover; cook on LOW 4 to 5 hours.

Pasta & Grains

Bolognese over Rigatoni

makes 4 to 6 servings

1 **pound ground beef**
⅓ **cup finely chopped onion**
⅓ **cup finely chopped carrot**
⅓ **cup finely chopped celery**
3 **cloves garlic, minced**
1 **can (about 28 ounces) diced tomatoes with basil, garlic and oregano**
½ **teaspoon salt**
½ **teaspoon black pepper**
½ **cup grated Pecorino Romano cheese**
8 **ounces uncooked rigatoni**
 Shaved Pecorino Romano cheese (optional)
 Chopped fresh basil (optional)

1. Cook beef, onion, carrot and celery in large skillet over medium-high heat 6 to 8 minutes or until beef is no longer pink, stirring to break up meat. Stir in garlic; cook 1 minute. Remove beef mixture to **Crockpot™** slow cooker using slotted spoon. Stir in tomatoes, salt and pepper. Cover; cook on LOW 6½ to 7 hours or on HIGH 3½ to 4 hours.

2. Stir grated cheese into sauce. Cook, uncovered, on HIGH 20 minutes or until slightly thickened.

3. Meanwhile, cook pasta in large saucepan of salted boiling water according to package directions; drain. Divide pasta among serving bowls. Top with sauce, shaved cheese and basil, if desired.

Quinoa Pilaf with Shallot Vinaigrette

makes 6 servings

2 cups vegetable broth

1 cup uncooked quinoa, rinsed in fine-mesh strainer

2 stalks celery, finely chopped

1 carrot, finely chopped

½ small red onion, finely chopped

½ teaspoon salt

¼ teaspoon dried thyme

1 medium shallot, chopped

1 tablespoon white wine vinegar

2 teaspoons honey

1 teaspoon Dijon mustard

⅛ teaspoon black pepper

¼ cup extra virgin olive oil

Chopped fresh parsley (optional)

1. Combine broth, quinoa, celery, carrot, onion, salt and thyme in **Crockpot**™ slow cooker. Cover; cook on HIGH 2 to 3 hours or until liquid is absorbed.

2. Meanwhile for vinaigrette, combine shallot, vinegar, honey, mustard and pepper in small bowl; whisk in oil. Fluff quinoa with fork; stir in vinaigrette. Garnish with parsley.

Cheesy Polenta

makes 6 servings

6 cups vegetable broth
1½ cups uncooked medium-grind
    instant polenta
½ cup grated Parmesan cheese
¼ cup (½ stick) butter, cubed
    Salt and black pepper
    Fried sage leaves (optional,
    see Tip)

1. Coat inside of **Crockpot**™ slow cooker with nonstick cooking spray. Bring broth to a boil in large saucepan over high heat. Pour into **Crockpot**™ slow cooker; whisk in polenta.

2. Cover; cook on LOW 2 to 2½ hours or until polenta is tender and creamy. Stir in cheese and butter. Season with salt and pepper. Garnish with fried sage.

Tip: To fry sage, melt 2 tablespoons butter in small skillet over medium heat. Add fresh sage leaves; cook until browned and crisp. Drain on paper towel-lined plate. Drizzle any remaining butter from skillet over polenta.

Arroz con Queso

makes 8 to 10 servings

1 can (about 14 ounces) crushed
   tomatoes

1 can (about 15 ounces) black
   beans, rinsed and drained

1½ cups uncooked converted long
    grain rice

1 onion, chopped

1 cup cottage cheese

1 can (4 ounces) chopped mild
   green chiles

2 tablespoons vegetable oil

3 teaspoons minced garlic

½ teaspoon salt

2 cups (8 ounces) shredded
   Monterey Jack cheese,
   divided

   Sliced jalapeño pepper
   (optional)

1. Combine tomatoes, beans, rice, onion, cottage cheese, chiles, oil, garlic and salt in **Crockpot™** slow cooker. Stir in 1 cup Monterey Jack cheese. Cover; cook on LOW 6 to 9 hours or until liquid is absorbed and rice is tender.

2. Sprinkle with remaining 1 cup Monterey Jack cheese; let stand until melted. Garnish with jalapeño pepper.

Macaroni and Cheese

makes 6 to 8 servings

6 **cups hot cooked elbow macaroni***

2 **tablespoons butter**

6 **cups (24 ounces) shredded Cheddar cheese**

4 **cups evaporated milk**

2 **teaspoons salt**

½ **teaspoon black pepper**

*Cook pasta 2 minutes less than the package directs for al dente.

Combine macaroni and butter in **Crockpot**™ slow cooker; stir until butter is melted. Stir in cheese, evaporated milk, salt and pepper. Cover; cook on HIGH 2 to 3 hours.

Tip: Make this macaroni and cheese recipe even better by adding some mix-ins. Diced green or red bell pepper, peas, hot dog slices, chopped tomato, browned ground beef or chopped onion are all great options.

Wild Rice and Dried Cherry Risotto

makes 8 to 10 servings

1 cup dry-roasted salted peanuts
6 teaspoons sesame oil, divided
1 cup chopped onion
6 ounces uncooked wild rice
1 cup diced carrots
1 cup chopped green or red bell pepper
½ cup dried cherries
⅛ to ¼ teaspoon red pepper flakes
4 cups hot water
¼ cup teriyaki or soy sauce
1 teaspoon salt

1. Coat inside of **Crockpot**™ slow cooker with nonstick cooking spray. Heat large skillet over medium-high heat. Add peanuts; cook and stir 2 to 3 minutes or until lightly browned. Remove to plate; set aside.

2. Heat 2 teaspoons oil in same skillet. Add onion; cook and stir 6 minutes or until softened and lightly browned. Remove to **Crockpot**™ slow cooker. Stir in rice, carrots, bell pepper, cherries, red pepper flakes and water. Cover; cook on HIGH 3 hours.

3. Turn off heat. Let stand 15 minutes, uncovered, until liquid is absorbed. Stir in teriyaki sauce, peanuts, remaining 4 teaspoons oil and salt.

Classic Beef and Noodles

makes 8 servings

1 tablespoon vegetable oil
2 pounds cubed beef stew meat
4 ounces mushrooms, sliced
2 tablespoons chopped onion
2 cloves garlic, minced
1 teaspoon salt
1 teaspoon dried oregano
½ teaspoon black pepper
¼ teaspoon dried marjoram
1 bay leaf
1½ cups beef broth
⅓ cup dry sherry
1 container (8 ounces) sour cream
½ cup all-purpose flour
¼ cup water
Hot cooked egg noodles

1. Heat oil in large skillet over medium heat. Add beef in batches; cook until browned on all sides, turning occasionally. Drain fat.

2. Combine beef, mushrooms, onion, garlic, salt, oregano, pepper, marjoram and bay leaf in **Crockpot**™ slow cooker. Pour in broth and sherry. Cover; cook on LOW 8 to 10 hours or on HIGH 4 to 5 hours. Remove and discard bay leaf.

3. Combine sour cream, flour and water in medium bowl. Whisk about 1 cup cooking liquid from **Crockpot**™ slow cooker into sour cream mixture. Stir mixture into **Crockpot**™ slow cooker. Cook, uncovered, on HIGH 30 minutes or until thickened and bubbly. Serve over noodles.

Spinach Risotto

makes 4 servings

- **2 tablespoons butter**
- **2 tablespoons olive oil**
- **¼ cup finely chopped shallot**
- **1¼ cups uncooked Arborio rice**
- **½ cup dry white wine**
- **3 cups vegetable broth**
- **½ teaspoon salt**
- **2 cups baby spinach**
- **¼ cup grated Parmesan cheese**
- **2 tablespoons pine nuts, toasted***

*To toast pine nuts, spread in single layer in heavy skillet. Cook and stir over medium heat 1 to 2 minutes or until nuts are lightly browned.

1. Melt butter in medium skillet over medium heat; add oil. Add shallot; cook and stir until softened but not browned.

2. Stir in rice; cook 2 minutes or until well coated. Stir in wine; cook until reduced by half. Remove to **Crockpot**™ slow cooker. Add broth and salt; mix well. Cover; cook on HIGH 2 to 2½ hours or until rice is al dente and still contains a little liquid.

3. Stir in spinach. Cover; cook on HIGH 15 to 20 minutes or until rice is tender and creamy. Stir in cheese and pine nuts just before serving.

Vegetable Mains & Sides

Mashed Rutabagas and Potatoes

makes 8 servings

2 pounds rutabagas, peeled and cut into ½-inch pieces

1 pound potatoes, peeled and cut into ½-inch pieces

½ cup milk

2 tablespoons chopped fresh parsley

½ teaspoon ground nutmeg

Salt and black pepper

1. Place rutabagas and potatoes in **Crockpot**™ slow cooker; add enough water to cover vegetables. Cover; cook on LOW 6 hours or on HIGH 3 hours or until vegetables are very tender. Remove vegetables to large bowl using slotted spoon. Discard cooking liquid.

2. Mash vegetables with potato masher to desired consistency. Stir in milk, parsley, nutmeg, salt and pepper.

Orange-Spiced Glazed Carrots >>
makes 6 servings

1 package (32 ounces) baby
   carrots
½ cup packed brown sugar
½ cup orange juice
1 tablespoon butter
¾ teaspoon ground cinnamon
¼ teaspoon ground nutmeg
¼ cup cold water
2 tablespoons cornstarch

1. Combine carrots, brown sugar, orange juice, butter, cinnamon and nutmeg in **Crockpot**™ slow cooker; stir to blend. Cover; cook on LOW 3½ to 4 hours. Remove carrots to large serving bowl using slotted spoon.

2. Turn **Crockpot**™ slow cooker to HIGH. Stir water into cornstarch in small bowl until smooth; whisk into cooking liquid. Cover; cook on HIGH 15 minutes or until thickened. Spoon sauce over carrots.

Gratin Potatoes with Asiago Cheese
makes 4 to 6 servings

6 slices bacon, cut into 1-inch
   pieces
6 medium baking potatoes,
   peeled and thinly sliced
   Salt and black pepper
½ cup grated Asiago cheese
1½ cups whipping cream

1. Heat large skillet over medium heat. Add bacon; cook and stir until crisp. Remove to paper towel-lined plate using slotted spoon.

2. Pour bacon drippings into **Crockpot**™ slow cooker. Layer one fourth of potatoes on bottom of **Crockpot**™ slow cooker. Season with salt and pepper. Sprinkle one fourth of bacon over potatoes and top with one fourth of cheese.

3. Repeat layers three times. Pour cream over all. Cover; cook on LOW 7 to 9 hours or on HIGH 5 to 6 hours.

Thai Red Curry with Tofu

makes 4 servings

1 medium sweet potato, peeled and cut into 1-inch pieces

1 small eggplant, halved lengthwise and cut crosswise into ½-inch slices

8 ounces extra firm tofu, cut into 1-inch pieces

½ cup cut green beans (1-inch pieces)

½ red bell pepper, cut into ¼-inch strips

2 tablespoons vegetable oil

5 medium shallots, thinly sliced (about 1½ cups)

3 tablespoons Thai red curry paste

1 teaspoon minced garlic

1 teaspoon grated ginger

1 can (about 13 ounces) unsweetened coconut milk

1½ tablespoons soy sauce

1 tablespoon packed brown sugar

¼ cup chopped fresh basil

2 tablespoons lime juice

Hot cooked rice (optional)

1. Coat inside of **Crockpot**™ slow cooker with nonstick cooking spray. Add sweet potato, eggplant, tofu, green beans and bell pepper.

2. Heat oil in large skillet over medium heat. Add shallots; cook 5 minutes or until browned and tender. Add curry paste, garlic and ginger; cook and stir 1 minute. Add coconut milk, soy sauce and brown sugar; bring to a simmer. Pour mixture over vegetables in **Crockpot**™ slow cooker.

3. Cover; cook on LOW 2 to 3 hours. Stir in basil and lime juice. Serve with rice, if desired.

Black Bean, Zucchini and Corn Enchiladas

makes 6 servings

1 tablespoon vegetable oil
1 medium onion, chopped
2 medium zucchini, chopped
2 cups corn
1 large red bell pepper, chopped
1 teaspoon minced garlic
½ teaspoon salt
½ teaspoon ground cumin
¼ teaspoon ground coriander
1 can (about 15 ounces) black
 beans, rinsed and drained
3 cups salsa verde
12 (6-inch) corn tortillas
2½ cups (10 ounces) shredded
 Monterey Jack cheese
2 tablespoons chopped fresh
 cilantro

1. Heat oil in large skillet over medium heat. Add onion; cook and stir 6 minutes or until softened. Add zucchini, corn and bell pepper; cook and stir 2 minutes. Add garlic, salt, cumin and coriander; cook and stir 1 minute. Stir in beans. Remove from heat.

2. Pour 1 cup salsa in bottom of **Crockpot™** slow cooker. Arrange 3 tortillas in single layer, cutting the tortillas in half as needed to make them fit. Place 2 cups vegetable mixture over tortillas; sprinkle with ½ cup cheese. Repeat layering two more times. Layer with remaining 3 tortillas; top with 2 cups salsa. Sprinkle with remaining 1 cup cheese. Reserve remaining filling for another use.

3. Cover; cook on HIGH 2 hours or until cheese is bubbly and edges are lightly browned. Sprinkle with cilantro. Turn off heat. Let stand, uncovered, 10 minutes before serving.

Frijoles Borrachos

makes 8 servings

6 slices bacon, chopped

1 medium yellow onion, chopped

1 tablespoon minced garlic

3 jalapeño peppers, seeded and finely diced*

1 tablespoon dried oregano

1 can (12 ounces) beer

6 cups water

1 pound dried pinto beans, rinsed and sorted

1 can (about 14 ounces) diced tomatoes

1 tablespoon salt

¼ cup chopped fresh cilantro

Jalapeño peppers can sting and irritate the skin, so wear rubber gloves when handling peppers and do not touch your eyes.

1. Heat large skillet over medium-high heat. Add bacon; cook 5 minutes or until mostly browned and crisp. Remove to **Crockpot**™ slow cooker using slotted spoon. Discard all but 3 tablespoons of drippings.

2. Heat same skillet over medium heat. Add onion; cook and stir 6 minutes or until softened and lightly browned. Add garlic, jalapeño peppers and oregano; cook 30 seconds or until fragrant. *Increase heat to medium-high.* Add beer; bring to a simmer. Cook 2 minutes, stirring to scrape up any browned bits from bottom of skillet. Remove mixture to **Crockpot**™ slow cooker.

3. Add water, beans, tomatoes and salt to **Crockpot**™ slow cooker. Cover; cook on LOW 7 hours or on HIGH 3 to 4 hours. Mash beans slightly until broth is thickened and creamy. Top with cilantro.

Zoodles in Tomato Sauce

makes 4 servings

1 can (28 ounces) diced tomatoes

1 can (6 ounces) tomato paste

2 tablespoons chopped onion

2 teaspoons minced garlic

1 teaspoon salt

½ teaspoon dried oregano

½ teaspoon dried basil

2 large zucchini (about 16 ounces *each*), ends trimmed and cut into 3-inch pieces

¼ cup shredded Parmesan cheese (optional)

1. Coat inside of **Crockpot**™ slow cooker with nonstick cooking spray. Add diced tomatoes, tomato paste, onion, garlic, salt, oregano and basil; stir to blend. Cover; cook on HIGH 3 hours.

2. Meanwhile, cut zucchini into ribbons with fine spiral blade of spiralizer.* Add zucchini to **Crockpot**™ slow cooker. Cover; cook on HIGH 30 minutes or until zucchini is tender. Top with cheese, if desired.

If you don't have a spiralizer, cut the zucchini into ribbons with a mandoline or sharp knife. Or purchase 2 pounds of prepared zucchini noodles from the produce section of the supermarket.

German Potato Salad >>

makes 6 servings

8 slices bacon
1 medium onion, chopped
3 stalks celery, chopped
2 pounds small red potatoes, cut into ¼-inch slices
1 cup chicken broth
¼ cup cider vinegar
   Salt and black pepper

1. Heat large skillet over medium heat. Add bacon; cook and stir until crisp. Remove to paper towel-lined plate using tongs; chop when cool enough to handle. Place bacon in small bowl; refrigerate until ready to serve.

2. Heat drippings in same skillet over medium-high heat. Add onion and celery; cook and stir 6 to 8 minutes or until onion is softened.

3. Layer half of potatoes and half of onion mixture in **Crockpot**™ slow cooker; repeat layers. Top with broth. Cover; cook on HIGH 4 hours.

4. Stir in vinegar, bacon, salt and pepper.

Collard Greens

makes 12 servings

1 tablespoon olive oil
3 turkey necks
5 bunches collard greens, stemmed and chopped
5 cups chicken broth
1 small onion, chopped
2 cloves garlic, minced
1 tablespoon cider vinegar
1 teaspoon sugar
   Salt and black pepper
   Red pepper flakes (optional)

1. Heat oil in large skillet over medium-high heat. Add turkey necks; cook 3 to 5 minutes or until browned, turning occasionally.

2. Combine turkey necks, collard greens, broth, onion and garlic in **Crockpot**™ slow cooker; stir to blend. Cover; cook on LOW 5 to 6 hours. Remove and discard turkey necks. Stir in vinegar, sugar, salt, black pepper and red pepper flakes, if desired.

Spinach Gorgonzola Corn Bread >>

makes 1 loaf

2 boxes (8½ ounces *each*) corn bread mix

1 package (10 ounces) frozen chopped spinach, thawed and drained

1 package (5 ounces) crumbled Gorgonzola cheese

3 eggs

½ cup whipping cream

½ teaspoon black pepper

1. Coat inside of 5-quart **Crockpot**™ slow cooker with nonstick cooking spray. Combine corn bread mix, spinach, cheese, eggs, cream and pepper in medium bowl; stir to blend. Pour batter into **Crockpot**™ slow cooker.

2. Cover; cook on HIGH 1½ hours. Turn off heat. Let bread cool completely before inverting onto large serving platter.

Note: Cook only on HIGH setting for proper crust and texture.

Cheesy Mashed Potato Casserole

makes 10 to 12 servings

4 pounds Yukon Gold potatoes, peeled and cut into 1-inch pieces

2 cups vegetable broth

3 tablespoons butter, cubed

½ cup milk, heated

⅓ cup sour cream

2 cups (8 ounces) shredded sharp Cheddar cheese

½ teaspoon salt

¼ teaspoon black pepper

1. Coat inside of **Crockpot**™ slow cooker with nonstick cooking spray. Add potatoes and broth; dot with butter. Cover; cook on LOW 4½ to 5 hours.

2. Mash potatoes with potato masher; stir in milk, sour cream, cheese, salt and pepper until cheese is melted.

Portobello Bolognese Sauce

makes 4 servings

2 tablespoons olive oil

2 cups (6 to 8 ounces) chopped portobello mushrooms

4 cloves garlic, minced

1 jar (24 to 26 ounces) spicy pasta sauce

1 cup thinly sliced carrots

2 tablespoons tomato paste

8 ounces uncooked spaghetti

½ cup shredded Parmesan or Romano cheese

¼ cup shredded fresh basil

1. Coat inside of **Crockpot**™ slow cooker with nonstick cooking spray. Heat oil in large skillet over medium heat. Add mushrooms and garlic; cook 6 minutes or until mushrooms have released their liquid, stirring occasionally.

2. Combine mushroom mixture, pasta sauce, carrots and tomato paste in **Crockpot**™ slow cooker; stir to blend. Cover; cook on LOW 5 to 6 hours or on HIGH 2½ to 3 hours or until sauce has thickened and carrots are tender.

3. Cook spaghetti in large saucepan of salted boiling water according to package directions; drain. Divide spaghetti among serving bowls; top with sauce, cheese and basil.

Artichoke and Tomato Paella

makes 8 servings

4 cups vegetable broth

2 cups uncooked converted rice

½ (10-ounce) package frozen chopped spinach, thawed and squeezed dry

1 green bell pepper, chopped

1 medium tomato, sliced into wedges

1 medium yellow onion, chopped

1 medium carrot, diced

3 cloves garlic, minced

1 tablespoon minced fresh parsley

Salt and black pepper

1 can (13¾ ounces) artichoke hearts, quartered, rinsed and well drained

½ cup frozen peas, thawed

Combine broth, rice, spinach, bell pepper, tomato, onion, carrot, garlic, parsley, salt and black pepper in **Crockpot**™ slow cooker; mix well. Cover; cook on LOW 4 hours or on HIGH 2 hours. Stir in artichoke hearts and peas. Cover; cook on HIGH 15 minutes.

Sandwiches & Tacos

Italian Meatball Hoagies

makes 4 servings

8 ounces ground beef

8 ounces Italian sausage, casings removed

¼ cup seasoned dry bread crumbs

¼ cup grated Parmesan cheese, plus additional for topping

1 egg

1 tablespoon olive oil

1 cup pasta sauce

2 tablespoons tomato paste

¼ teaspoon red pepper flakes (optional)

4 (6-inch) hoagie rolls, split

1. Coat inside of **Crockpot**™ slow cooker with nonstick cooking spray. Combine beef, sausage, bread crumbs, ¼ cup cheese and egg in large bowl; mix well. Shape into 12 (1½-inch) meatballs.

2. Heat oil in large skillet over medium heat. Add meatballs; cook 6 to 8 minutes or until browned on all sides, turning occasionally. Remove meatballs to **Crockpot**™ slow cooker using slotted spoon.

3. Combine pasta sauce, tomato paste and red pepper flakes, if desired, in medium bowl; stir to blend. Spoon over meatballs; stir gently.

4. Cover; cook on LOW 5 to 7 hours or on HIGH 2½ to 3 hours. Place meatballs in rolls. Spoon sauce over meatballs; top with additional cheese.

Lentil Sloppy Joes

makes 6 servings

1 can (about 15 ounces) tomato sauce

1 cup dried lentils, rinsed and sorted

1 cup vegetable broth

1 medium onion, chopped

1 medium bell pepper, chopped

3 tablespoons sugar

1 tablespoon chili powder

1 teaspoon salt

½ teaspoon garlic powder

½ teaspoon onion powder

Whole wheat hamburger buns, toasted

Optional toppings: avocado slices, shredded cheese, onion slices and/or pickles

Combine tomato sauce, lentils, broth, onion, bell pepper, sugar, chili powder, salt, garlic powder and onion powder in **Crockpot**™ slow cooker; stir to blend. Cover; cook on HIGH 4 hours or until lentils are tender. Serve on buns. Top as desired.

Hot Beef Sandwiches au Jus

makes 8 to 10 servings

4 pounds boneless beef bottom round roast, trimmed*

2 cans (about 10 ounces *each*) condensed beef broth, undiluted

1 can (12 ounces) beer

2 envelopes (1 ounce *each*) onion soup mix

1 tablespoon minced garlic

2 teaspoons sugar

1 teaspoon dried oregano

Crusty French rolls, sliced in half

*Unless you have a 5-, 6- or 7-quart Crockpot™ slow cooker, cut any roast larger than 2½ pounds in half so it cooks completely.

1. Place beef in **Crockpot**™ slow cooker. Combine broth, beer, dry soup mix, garlic, sugar and oregano in large bowl; stir to blend. Pour mixture over beef. Cover; cook on HIGH 6 to 8 hours.

2. Remove beef to large cutting board; shred with two forks. Return beef to cooking liquid; stir to blend. Serve on rolls with cooking liquid for dipping.

Chicken and Spicy Black Bean Tacos

makes 6 servings

1 can (about 15 ounces) black beans, rinsed and drained

1 can (10 ounces) diced tomatoes with green chiles, drained

1½ teaspoons chili powder

¾ teaspoon ground cumin

¼ to ½ teaspoon ground red pepper

1 teaspoon olive oil

12 ounces boneless, skinless chicken breasts

12 hard corn taco shells

Optional toppings: shredded lettuce, diced tomatoes, shredded Cheddar cheese, sour cream and/or sliced black olives

1. Coat inside of **Crockpot™** slow cooker with nonstick cooking spray. Add beans and tomatoes. Combine chili powder, cumin, ground red pepper and oil in small bowl; rub all over chicken. Place chicken in **Crockpot™** slow cooker. Cover; cook on HIGH 1 to 2 hours.

2. Remove chicken to large cutting board; cut into ½-inch slices when cool enough to handle. Remove bean mixture to large bowl using slotted spoon.

3. To serve, warm taco shells according to package directions. Fill with bean mixture and chicken. Top as desired.

Cheeseburger Sloppy Joes

makes 8 servings

3 pounds ground beef
1 medium onion, chopped
3 cloves garlic, minced
1 cup ketchup
½ cup water
2 tablespoons packed brown sugar
2 teaspoons Worcestershire sauce
4 cups (16 ounces) shredded sharp Cheddar cheese
8 hamburger buns

1. Coat inside of **Crockpot**™ slow cooker with nonstick cooking spray. Brown beef in large skillet over medium-high heat 6 to 8 minutes, stirring to break up meat. Drain fat. Remove beef to **Crockpot**™ slow cooker.

2. Heat same skillet over medium-high heat. Add onion and garlic; cook and stir 5 minutes or until onion is softened. Remove onion mixture to **Crockpot**™ slow cooker.

3. Add ketchup, water, brown sugar and Worcestershire sauce to **Crockpot**™ slow cooker; stir to blend. Cover; cook on HIGH 2 to 2½ hours. Stir in cheese until melted. Serve on buns.

Ancho Chile and Lime Pork Tacos

makes 10 to 12 servings

2 large plantain leaves

1 boneless pork shoulder roast
(4 to 6 pounds)*

Juice of 5 limes

1 package (about 1 ounce) ancho
chile paste

Salt

1 large onion, sliced

Pickled Red Onions (recipe
follows)

Cilantro-Lime Rice (recipe
follows, optional)

Flour tortillas

Lime slices (optional)

*Unless you have a 5-, 6- or 7-quart
Crockpot™ slow cooker, cut any roast
larger than 2½ pounds in half so it
cooks completely.*

1. Line **Crockpot**™ slow cooker with plantain leaves; top with pork. Combine lime juice, chile paste and salt in medium bowl until well blended. Add paste mixture and onion to **Crockpot**™ slow cooker; wrap leaves over pork. Cover; cook on LOW 8 to 10 hours.

2. Meanwhile, prepare Pickled Red Onions and Cilantro-Lime Rice, if desired.

3. Serve pork in tortillas; top with Pickled Red Onions. Serve with lime slices and Cilantro-Lime Rice, if desired.

Pickled Red Onions: Combine 1 cup sliced red onion, juice of 2 limes, ¼ teaspoon sugar and ¼ teaspoon salt in small bowl; set aside until ready to use. Makes 1 cup.

Cilantro-Lime Rice: Prepare 2 cups rice according to package directions. Stir in ¼ cup butter, ½ cup chopped fresh cilantro, juice of 4 limes and 1 teaspoon salt.

Barbecue Beef Sliders

makes 12 sliders

1 tablespoon packed brown sugar

1 teaspoon ground cumin

1 teaspoon chili powder

1 teaspoon paprika

½ teaspoon salt

¼ teaspoon ground red pepper

3 pounds beef short ribs

½ cup plus 2 tablespoons barbecue sauce, divided

¼ cup water

12 slider rolls

¾ cup prepared coleslaw

12 pickle slices

1. Coat inside of **Crockpot**™ slow cooker with nonstick cooking spray. Combine brown sugar, cumin, chili powder, paprika, salt and ground red pepper in small bowl; toss to blend. Rub all over ribs; remove to **Crockpot**™ slow cooker. Pour in ½ cup barbecue sauce and water; turn to coat ribs.

2. Cover; cook on LOW 7 to 8 hours or on HIGH 4 to 4½ hours or until ribs are very tender and meat shreds easily. Remove ribs to large cutting board. Discard bones; remove meat to large bowl. Shred meat using two forks, discarding any large pieces of fat. Stir in remaining 2 tablespoons barbecue sauce and 2 tablespoons liquid from **Crockpot**™ slow cooker.

3. Fill each roll with ¼ cup beef mixture, 1 tablespoon coleslaw and 1 pickle slice.

Tofu, Black Bean and Corn Chili Burritos

makes 10 servings

1 can (about 15 ounces) black beans, rinsed and drained

1 can (about 14 ounces) diced tomatoes with green pepper, celery and onion

8 ounces firm tofu, crumbled

1 cup mild prepared salsa

¾ cup vegetable broth or water

½ cup corn

½ cup uncooked long grain rice

1 tablespoon chili powder

1 teaspoon ground cumin

1 teaspoon salt

¼ teaspoon ground chipotle pepper

½ teaspoon dried oregano

20 small or 10 large flour tortillas

Optional toppings: sliced avocado, sour cream, lettuce and/or chopped fresh cilantro

1. Combine beans, tomatoes, tofu, salsa, broth, corn, rice, chili powder, cumin, salt, chipotle pepper and oregano in **Crockpot**™ slow cooker; stir to blend. Cover; cook on LOW 8 hours or on HIGH 4 hours.

2. Top each tortilla with bean mixture and desired toppings. Fold short ends of each tortilla over part of filling then roll up.

Pulled Pork Sliders with Cola Barbecue Sauce

makes 16 sliders

1 boneless pork shoulder roast (3 pounds)*

Salt

1 tablespoon vegetable oil

1 cup cola

¼ cup tomato paste

2 tablespoons packed brown sugar

2 teaspoons Worcestershire sauce

2 teaspoons spicy brown mustard

Hot pepper sauce

16 dinner rolls or potato rolls, split

Sliced pickles (optional)

Unless you have a 5-, 6- or 7-quart Crockpot™ slow cooker, cut any roast larger than 2½ pounds in half so it cooks completely.

1. Season pork all over with salt. Heat oil in large skillet over medium-high heat. Add pork; cook 5 to 7 minutes or until browned on all sides. Remove to **Crockpot™** slow cooker. Pour cola over pork. Cover; cook on LOW 7½ to 8 hours or on HIGH 3½ to 4 hours.

2. Turn off heat. Remove pork to large cutting board; shred with two forks. Let cooking liquid stand 5 minutes. Skim off and discard fat. Turn **Crockpot™** slow cooker to HIGH. Whisk tomato paste, brown sugar, Worcestershire sauce and mustard into cooking liquid. Cover; cook on HIGH 15 minutes or until thickened.

3. Stir shredded pork back into **Crockpot™** slow cooker. Season with hot pepper sauce and salt. Serve on rolls. Top with pickles, if desired.

Appetizers & Dips

Feta and Mint Spread

makes about 1 cup

½ **cup plain Greek yogurt**
3 **ounces feta cheese, crumbled**
2 **ounces cream cheese, cubed**
2 **tablespoons extra virgin olive oil**
1 **small clove garlic, minced**
  Baked Pita Chips (page 158)
1 **tablespoon chopped fresh mint**
½ **teaspoon grated lemon peel**

1. Coat inside of **Crockpot**™ "No Dial" food warmer with nonstick cooking spray. Add yogurt, feta cheese, cream cheese, oil and garlic; mix well. Cover; heat 1 hour or until cheese is melted.

2. Meanwhile, prepare Baked Pita Chips.

3. Stir in mint and lemon peel. Serve dip with Baked Pita Chips.

Spicy Sweet and Sour Cocktail Franks >>

makes 10 to 12 servings

2 **packages (8 ounces** *each***) cocktail franks**
½ **cup ketchup or chili sauce**
½ **cup apricot preserves**
1 **teaspoon hot pepper sauce**

Combine cocktail franks, ketchup, preserves and hot pepper sauce in 1½-quart **Crockpot™** "No Dial" food warmer; mix well. Cover; heat 2 to 3 hours.

Baked Pita Chips

makes 36 chips

3 **pita bread rounds**
1 **tablespoon olive oil**
½ **teaspoon dried oregano**
¼ **teaspoon ground cumin**
⅛ **teaspoon salt**

1. Preheat oven to 375°F. Spray large baking sheet with nonstick cooking spray.

2. Brush one side of each pita round with oil. Sprinkle with oregano, cumin and salt. Cut each pita round into 12 wedges. Place on prepared baking sheet seasoned side up.

3. Bake 8 minutes or until lightly browned. Cool.

Caramelized Onion Dip >>
makes 1½ cups

1 tablespoon olive oil
1½ cups chopped sweet onion
1 teaspoon sugar
⅛ teaspoon dried thyme
¼ teaspoon salt
2 ounces cream cheese, cubed
½ cup sour cream
⅓ cup mayonnaise
⅓ cup shredded Swiss cheese
¼ teaspoon beef bouillon
    granules
Potato chips and carrot sticks

1. Heat oil in medium skillet over medium heat. Add onion, sugar and thyme; cook 12 minutes or until golden, stirring occasionally. Stir in salt.

2. Coat inside of **Crockpot™** "No Dial" food warmer with nonstick cooking spray. Add onion mixture, cream cheese, sour cream, mayonnaise, Swiss cheese and bouillon granules; mix well. Cover; heat 1 hour or until warm. Stir to blend. Serve with potato chips and carrot sticks.

Pepperoni Pizza Dip
makes 1⅓ cups

1 jar (about 14 ounces) pizza
    sauce
⅓ cup chopped pepperoni
½ can (about 2¼ ounces) sliced
    black olives, drained
1 teaspoon dried oregano
½ cup (2 ounces) shredded
    mozzarella cheese
4 ounces cream cheese, softened
Bread sticks

1. Combine pizza sauce, pepperoni, olives and oregano in 2-quart **Crockpot™** slow cooker. Cover; cook on LOW 2 hours or on HIGH 1 to 1½ hours or until mixture is heated through.

2. Stir in mozzarella cheese and cream cheese until melted and well blended. Serve with bread sticks for dipping.

Cereal Snack Mix >>

makes 20 servings

- 6 **tablespoons (¾ stick) butter, melted**
- 2 **tablespoons curry powder**
- 2 **tablespoons soy sauce**
- 1 **tablespoon sugar**
- 1 **tablespoon paprika**
- 2 **teaspoons ground cumin**
- ½ **teaspoon salt**
- 5 **cups rice cereal squares**
- 5 **cups corn cereal squares**
- 1 **cup tiny pretzels**
- ⅓ **cup peanuts**

1. Pour butter into **Crockpot**™ slow cooker. Stir in curry powder, soy sauce, sugar, paprika, cumin and salt. Stir in cereal, pretzels and peanuts. Cook, uncovered, on HIGH 45 minutes, stirring often.

2. Turn **Crockpot**™ slow cooker to LOW. Cook, uncovered, on LOW 3 to 4 hours, stirring often. Turn off heat. Let cool completely.

Chipotle Chili con Queso Dip

makes 1½ cups

- 10 **ounces pasteurized process cheese product, cubed**
- ¼ **cup mild chunky salsa**
- 1 to 2 **canned chipotle peppers in adobo sauce, finely chopped**
- ½ **teaspoon Worcestershire sauce**
- ⅛ **teaspoon chili powder**
  Tortilla chips or pretzels

1. Coat inside of **Crockpot**™ "No-Dial" food warmer with nonstick cooking spray. Combine cheese product, salsa, chipotle pepper, Worcestershire sauce and chili powder in **Crockpot**™ "No Dial" food warmer. Cover; heat 1 hour.

2. Stir well. Replace cover; heat 30 minutes or until cheese product is melted. Stir to blend. Serve with tortilla chips.

Honey-Glazed Chicken Wings >>
makes 6 servings

- 3 tablespoons vegetable oil, divided
- 3 pounds chicken wings
- 1 cup honey
- ½ cup soy sauce
- 2 tablespoons tomato paste
- 2 teaspoons water
- 1 clove garlic, minced
- 1 teaspoon sugar
- 1 teaspoon black pepper

1. Heat 1½ tablespoons oil in large skillet over medium heat. Add wings in batches; cook 3 to 5 minutes on each side or until browned. Remove to **Crockpot**™ slow cooker using tongs.

2. Combine remaining 1½ tablespoons oil, honey, soy sauce, tomato paste, water, garlic, sugar and pepper in medium bowl; stir to blend. Pour sauce over wings. Cover; cook on LOW 6 to 8 hours or on HIGH 3 to 4 hours.

Party Meatballs
makes 10 to 12 servings

- 1 package (about 1½ pounds) frozen cocktail-size turkey or beef meatballs
- ½ cup maple syrup
- 1 jar (12 ounces) chili sauce
- 1 jar (12 ounces) grape jelly

Place meatballs, maple syrup, chili sauce and jelly in **Crockpot**™ slow cooker; stir to blend. Cover; cook on LOW 3 to 4 hours or on HIGH 2 to 3 hours.

Refried Bean Dip with Blue Tortilla Chips >>

makes 10 servings

- 3 **cans (about 16 ounces *each*) refried beans**
- 1 **cup taco sauce**
- ½ **teaspoon salt**
- ½ **teaspoon black pepper**
- 3 **cups (12 ounces) shredded Cheddar cheese**
- ¾ **cup chopped green onions**
  Blue corn tortilla chips

1. Combine refried beans, taco sauce, salt and pepper in large bowl; stir to blend.

2. Spread one third of bean mixture on bottom of **Crockpot**™ slow cooker. Sprinkle evenly with ¾ cup cheese. Repeat layers two times, finishing with cheese layer. Sprinkle green onions evenly on cheese. Cover; cook on LOW 2 to 4 hours. Serve with tortilla chips.

Spicy Cheddar Dip

makes about 1½ cups

- 2 **slices bacon, chopped**
- 4 **ounces cream cheese, cubed**
- 1 **cup (4 ounces) shredded extra sharp Cheddar cheese**
- ½ **jalapeño pepper, finely chopped***
- ½ **teaspoon hot pepper sauce**
- 3 **tablespoons sour cream**
  Tortilla chips and/or pretzel sticks

*Jalapeño peppers can sting and irritate the skin, so wear rubber gloves when handling peppers and do not touch your eyes.

1. Heat small skillet over medium heat. Add bacon; cook 4 minutes or until crisp, stirring occasionally. Remove with slotted spoon to paper towel-lined plate.

2. Coat inside of **Crockpot**™ "No Dial" food warmer with nonstick cooking spray. Combine cream cheese, Cheddar cheese, jalapeño pepper, hot pepper sauce and bacon in **Crockpot**™ "No Dial" food warmer. Cover; heat 1 hour.

3. Stir in sour cream. Cover; heat 30 minutes or until heated through and cheese is melted. Serve with tortilla chips.

Pepperoni Pizza Monkey Bread

makes 12 servings

1 package (about 3 ounces) pepperoni slices, divided

1 teaspoon minced garlic

¼ teaspoon red pepper flakes

1 can (about 16 ounces) refrigerated biscuits, each biscuit cut into 6 pieces

1 can (15 ounces) pizza sauce

1 small green bell pepper, chopped

2 cups (8 ounces) shredded mozzarella cheese

1. Prepare foil handles.* Coat inside of **Crockpot**™ slow cooker and foil handles with nonstick cooking spray.

2. Chop half of pepperoni slices. Combine chopped pepperoni, garlic and red pepper flakes in medium bowl. Roll each biscuit piece into pepperoni mixture; place in **Crockpot**™ slow cooker. Pour half of pizza sauce over dough; reserve remaining pizza sauce for dipping. Top sauce with bell pepper, cheese and remaining whole pepperoni slices.

3. Cover; cook on LOW 3 hours. Turn off heat. Let stand 10 to 15 minutes. Remove bread from **Crockpot**™ slow cooker using foil handles. Serve with remaining pizza sauce for dipping.

*Prepare foil handles by tearing off one 18-inch long piece of foil; fold in half lengthwise. Fold in half lengthwise again to create 18×3-inch strip. Repeat two times. Crisscross foil strips in spoke design; place in **Crockpot**™ slow cooker. Leave strips in during cooking so you can easily lift the cooked item out again when cooking is complete.

Rosemary-Olive Focaccia

makes 1 loaf

1 cup warm water (100° to 110°F)

3 tablespoons extra virgin olive oil

3 packets (¼ ounce *each*) active dry yeast

1 tablespoon sugar

3 cups all-purpose flour

½ cup pitted kalamata olives, chopped

1 tablespoon plus 1 to 2 teaspoons chopped fresh rosemary, divided

1 teaspoon salt

¼ teaspoon red pepper flakes

1. Combine water, oil, yeast and sugar in medium bowl; let stand 5 minutes.

2. Combine flour, olives, 1 tablespoon rosemary and salt in large bowl. Pour water mixture into flour mixture; stir until rough dough forms. Turn out dough onto floured surface; knead about 5 minutes or until smooth and elastic. Place dough in greased bowl; turn to grease top. Cover and let rise in warm place about 1½ hours or until doubled in size.

3. Punch down dough. Coat inside of oval 6-quart **Crockpot**™ slow cooker with nonstick cooking spray. Add dough; press down and stretch to fit. Sprinkle with remaining 1 to 2 teaspoons rosemary and red pepper flakes.

4. Cover; cook on HIGH 1½ to 2 hours or until dough is puffed and lightly browned on the sides. Remove to wire rack; let cool 10 minutes. Cut into wedges.

Desserts & Drinks

Bananas Foster

makes 12 servings

12 bananas, cut into quarters

1 cup flaked coconut

1 cup dark corn syrup

⅔ cup butter, melted

¼ cup lemon juice

2 teaspoons grated lemon peel

2 teaspoons rum

1 teaspoon ground cinnamon

½ teaspoon salt

12 slices prepared pound cake

1 quart vanilla ice cream

1. Combine bananas and coconut in **Crockpot**™ slow cooker. Combine corn syrup, butter, lemon juice, lemon peel, rum, cinnamon and salt in medium bowl; stir to blend. Pour over bananas.

2. Cover; cook on LOW 1 to 2 hours. To serve, arrange bananas on pound cake slices. Top with ice cream and warm sauce.

Hot Toddies >>

makes 10 servings

8 cups water

2 cups bourbon

¾ cup honey

⅔ cup lemon juice

1 (1-inch) piece fresh ginger, peeled and cut into 4 slices

1 whole cinnamon stick

Lemon slices (optional)

1. Combine water, bourbon, honey, lemon juice, ginger and cinnamon stick in **Crockpot**™ slow cooker; stir to blend. Cover; cook on HIGH 2 hours. Turn **Crockpot**™ slow cooker to WARM.

2. Remove and discard cinnamon stick and ginger pieces. Serve toddies in mugs; garnish with lemon slices.

Ginger Pear Cider

makes 8 to 10 servings

8 cups pear juice or cider

¾ cup lemon juice

¼ to ½ cup honey

10 whole cloves

2 cinnamon sticks, plus additional for garnish

8 (¼-inch) slices fresh ginger

1. Combine pear juice, lemon juice, honey, cloves, 2 cinnamon sticks and ginger in 5-quart **Crockpot**™ slow cooker.

2. Cover; cook on LOW 5 to 6 hours or on HIGH 2½ to 3 hours. Remove and discard cloves, cinnamon sticks and ginger before serving. Serve cider in mugs; garnish with additional cinnamon sticks.

Streusel Pound Cake

makes 6 to 8 servings

1 package (16 ounces) pound
    cake mix, plus ingredients to
    prepare mix
¼ cup packed brown sugar
1 tablespoon all-purpose flour
¼ cup chopped nuts
1 teaspoon ground cinnamon
    Fresh berries (optional)
    Powdered sugar (optional)

1. Coat inside of 5-quart **Crockpot**™ slow cooker with nonstick cooking spray. Prepare cake mix according to package directions; stir in brown sugar, flour, nuts and cinnamon. Pour batter into **Crockpot**™ slow cooker. Cover; cook on HIGH 1 to 2 hours or until toothpick inserted into center comes out clean.

2. Invert cake onto wire rack. Cut into wedges; serve with berries and dust with powdered sugar, if desired.

Fruit Ambrosia with Dumplings

makes 4 to 6 servings

4 cups fresh or frozen fruit, cut into 1-inch pieces*

½ cup plus 2 tablespoons granulated sugar, divided

½ cup warm apple or cran-apple juice

2 tablespoons quick-cooking tapioca

1 cup all-purpose flour

1¼ teaspoons baking powder

¼ teaspoon salt

3 tablespoons cold butter, cubed

½ cup milk

1 egg

2 tablespoons packed brown sugar

Vanilla ice cream or whipped cream (optional)

*Use strawberries, raspberries and/or peaches.

1. Combine fruit, ½ cup granulated sugar, juice and tapioca in **Crockpot**™ slow cooker. Cover; cook on LOW 5 to 6 hours or on HIGH 2½ to 3 hours or until thick sauce forms.

2. Combine flour, remaining 2 tablespoons granulated sugar, baking powder and salt in medium bowl. Cut in butter using pastry blender or fingertips until mixture resembles coarse crumbs. Whisk milk and egg in small bowl. Pour milk mixture into flour mixture. Stir until soft dough forms.

3. Drop dough by teaspoonfuls on top of fruit. Sprinkle with brown sugar. Cover; cook on HIGH 30 minutes to 1 hour or until toothpick inserted into centers of dumplings comes out clean.

4. Serve fruit and dumplings warm with ice cream, if desired.

Cinnamon Latté >>

makes 6 to 8 servings

6 cups double-strength brewed coffee*

2 cups half-and-half

1 cup sugar

1 teaspoon vanilla

3 whole cinnamon sticks, plus additional for garnish

Whipped cream (optional)

Double the amount of coffee grounds normally used to brew coffee. Or substitute 8 teaspoons instant coffee dissolved in 6 cups boiling water.

1. Combine coffee, half-and-half, sugar and vanilla in **Crockpot**™ slow cooker; stir to blend. Add 3 cinnamon sticks. Cover; cook on HIGH 3 hours.

2. Remove and discard cinnamon sticks. Serve coffee in mugs; garnish with additional cinnamon sticks and whipped cream.

Minted Hot Cocoa

makes 6 to 8 servings

6 cups milk

¾ cup semisweet chocolate pieces

½ cup sugar

½ cup unsweetened cocoa powder

1 teaspoon vanilla

½ teaspoon mint extract

10 fresh mint sprigs, tied together with kitchen string

Whipped cream (optional)

1. Combine milk, chocolate, sugar, cocoa, vanilla and mint extract in **Crockpot**™ slow cooker; stir to blend. Add 10 mint sprigs. Cover; cook on LOW 3 to 4 hours.

2. Uncover; remove and discard mint sprigs. Whisk cocoa mixture well; cover until ready to serve. Serve cocoa in mugs; garnish with whipped cream.

Sticky Caramel Pumpkin Cake

makes 8 servings

2 cups all-purpose flour

2 teaspoons baking powder

1 teaspoon baking soda

½ teaspoon salt

½ teaspoon pumpkin pie spice or ground cinnamon

1⅓ cups sugar

1 cup (2 sticks) butter, softened

4 eggs, at room temperature

1 can (15 ounces) pumpkin purée

1 jar (16 ounces) caramel topping

Vanilla ice cream (optional)

1. Coat inside of 5-quart **Crockpot**™ slow cooker with nonstick cooking spray.

2. Combine flour, baking powder, baking soda, salt and pumpkin pie spice in medium bowl. Beat sugar and butter in large bowl with electric mixer at high speed 3 minutes or until blended. Add eggs, one at a time, beating well after each addition. Beat in pumpkin. Beat in flour mixture at low speed just until blended. Spread evenly in **Crockpot**™ slow cooker.

3. Cover; cook on HIGH 2 to 2½ hours or until toothpick inserted into center of cake comes out clean. Run thin knife around edge of cake to loosen. Cut into wedges in stoneware or invert cake onto serving plate. Drizzle caramel topping over cake and serve with ice cream, if desired.

Serving Suggestion: For a fancier presentation, trim a sheet of waxed paper to fit the bottom of the stoneware. Spray the stoneware and paper with nonstick cooking spray. Proceed as above, but before drizzling with caramel sauce, place a large plate upside-down on top of the cake and invert the stoneware allowing the cake to slide out onto the plate. Peel waxed paper from bottom of cake, then invert onto large serving plate.

Mocha Supreme

makes 8 servings

2 quarts strong brewed coffee

½ cup instant hot chocolate beverage mix

1 whole cinnamon stick, broken in half

1 cup cold whipping cream

1 tablespoon powdered sugar

1. Place coffee, hot chocolate mix and cinnamon stick halves in **Crockpot**™ slow cooker; stir to blend. Cover; cook on HIGH 2 to 2½ hours or until heated through. Remove and discard cinnamon stick halves.

2. Beat cream in medium bowl with electric mixer on high speed until soft peaks form. Add powdered sugar; beat until stiff peaks form. Serve coffee in mugs; top with whipped cream.

Fudge and Cream Pudding Cake

makes 8 to 10 servings

1 cup all-purpose flour

1 cup packed dark brown sugar, divided

5 tablespoons unsweetened cocoa powder, divided

2 teaspoons baking powder

½ teaspoon ground cinnamon

⅛ teaspoon salt

1 cup whipping cream

1 tablespoon vegetable oil

1 teaspoon vanilla

1½ cups hot water

Whipped cream (optional)

1. Coat inside of 5-quart **Crockpot**™ slow cooker with nonstick cooking spray.

2. Combine flour, ½ cup brown sugar, 3 tablespoons cocoa, baking powder, cinnamon and salt in medium bowl. Add cream, oil and vanilla; stir just until blended. Pour batter into **Crockpot**™ slow cooker.

3. Combine hot water, remaining ½ cup brown sugar and remaining 2 tablespoons cocoa in medium bowl; stir to blend. Pour sauce over cake batter. *Do not stir.* Cover; cook on HIGH 2 hours. Turn off heat. Let stand 10 minutes.

4. Scoop cake and sauce into serving bowls. Serve with whipped cream, if desired.

Metric Conversion Chart

VOLUME MEASUREMENTS (dry)

⅛ teaspoon = 0.5 mL
¼ teaspoon = 1 mL
½ teaspoon = 2 mL
¾ teaspoon = 4 mL
1 teaspoon = 5 mL
1 tablespoon = 15 mL
2 tablespoons = 30 mL
¼ cup = 60 mL
⅓ cup = 75 mL
½ cup = 125 mL
⅔ cup = 150 mL
¾ cup = 175 mL
1 cup = 250 mL
2 cups = 1 pint = 500 mL
3 cups = 750 mL
4 cups = 1 quart = 1 L

VOLUME MEASUREMENTS (fluid)

1 fluid ounce (2 tablespoons) = 30 mL
4 fluid ounces (½ cup) = 125 mL
8 fluid ounces (1 cup) = 250 mL
12 fluid ounces (1½ cups) = 375 mL
16 fluid ounces (2 cups) = 500 mL

WEIGHTS (mass)

½ ounce = 15 g
1 ounce = 30 g
3 ounces = 90 g
4 ounces = 120 g
8 ounces = 225 g
10 ounces = 285 g
12 ounces = 360 g
16 ounces = 1 pound = 450 g

DIMENSIONS

1/16 inch = 2 mm
⅛ inch = 3 mm
¼ inch = 6 mm
½ inch = 1.5 cm
¾ inch = 2 cm
1 inch = 2.5 cm

OVEN TEMPERATURES

250°F = 120°C
275°F = 140°C
300°F = 150°C
325°F = 160°C
350°F = 180°C
375°F = 190°C
400°F = 200°C
425°F = 220°C
450°F = 230°C

BAKING PAN SIZES

Utensil	Size in Inches/Quarts	Metric Volume	Size in Centimeters
Baking or Cake Pan (square or rectangular)	8×8×2	2 L	20×20×5
	9×9×2	2.5 L	23×23×5
	12×8×2	3 L	30×20×5
	13×9×2	3.5 L	33×23×5
Loaf Pan	8×4×3	1.5 L	20×10×7
	9×5×3	2 L	23×13×7
Round Layer Cake Pan	8×1½	1.2 L	20×4
	9×1½	1.5 L	23×4
Pie Plate	8×1¼	750 mL	20×3
	9×1¼	1 L	23×3
Baking Dish or Casserole	1 quart	1 L	—
	1½ quart	1.5 L	—
	2 quart	2 L	—